HIT LIST

Frequently Challenged Books for

CHILDREN

Donna Reidy Pistolis
Editor

for the
Office for Intellectual Freedom
of the
American Library Association

American Library Association
Chicago and London
1996

Cover and text design: Dianne M. Rooney

Composition by Impressions Book and Journal Services, Inc.
in Sabon and Futura using a Penta MV9300

Printed on 50-pound Victor Offset, a pH-neutral stock,
and bound in 10-point C1S cover stock by Victor
Graphics, Inc.

The paper used in this publication meets the minimum
requirements of American National Standard for
Information Sciences—Permanence of Paper for
Printed Library Materials, ANSI Z39.48-1992. ∞

Library of Congress Cataloging-in-Publication Data

Pistolis, Donna Reidy.
    Hit list—frequently challenged books for children / Donna Reidy
Pistolis for the Office for Intellectual Freedom of the American
Library Association.
        p.   cm.
    ISBN 0-8389-3458-7
    1. Challenged books—United States—Bibliography.   2. Children's
literature, English—Bibliography.   I. American Library
Association. Office for Intellectual Freedom.
Z1019.P57   1996   96-5759
016.8088′99282

Printed in the United States of America.

00 99 98 97 96   5 4 3 2 1

CONTENTS

ACKNOWLEDGMENTS

Special thanks to April Judge, former manager of the ALSC's Born to Read project, whose assistance with the writing of the annotations helped me tremendously.

Thanks also go to Cynthia Robinson, Ivan Scott, Betty Sereno, and Bridget Sweeney, staff of the Office for Intellectual Freedom, who helped me at one time or another with this publication.

I also wish to thank Judith F. Krug, director of the Office for Intellectual Freedom, without whom none of this would have been possible.

Finally, I wish to thank my husband, Todd.

INTRODUCTION

Challenges to library and curricular materials are nothing new. Indeed, the ALA Office for Intellectual Freedom has received reports of more than 3,500 such attempts in the last five years. There is no question that censorship attempts are increasing. Nevertheless, my rule of thumb—based on research—is that for every incident reported, there are as many as four or five that, for one reason or another, are not reported. So in terms of statistics, these numbers, distressing as they are, still represent only the tip of the iceberg. The prospect of a challenge, however, is not something that needs to be feared or viewed with apprehension. In fact, some challenges actually prove to be a valuable learning experience for most of the parties involved.

It is my hope that this publication will assist you, whether this is your first challenge or your fiftieth. The books chosen for inclusion represent a broad range of children's books that have been challenged. For each title, the entry includes an annotation, examples of challenges, citations to reviews, articles about the book, background articles about the book or the author, awards and prizes the book has won, where to look for more information on the author, and sources that have recommended the book.

Whatever the title that is being challenged, please remember you can always call the Office for Intellectual Freedom for assistance.

Judith F. Krug
Director
Office for Intellectual Freedom

The Stupids Step Out

Boston, Mass.: Houghton Mifflin, 1974

The Stupid family and their dog, Kitty, have a fun-filled day as they engage in ridiculously incongruous antics such as taking a waterless bath wearing clothes, wearing the cat as a hat, eating mashed-potato and butterscotch-syrup sundaes, and visiting grandparents who fail to recognize them.

This first book about the Stupid family combines the witty, humorous writing style of Allard with the slapstick, zany pictures of well-known picture-book illustrator, James Marshall. The escapades of this "wild and crazy" family are continued by this winning author-illustrator team in *The Stupids Have a Ball* (1984), *The Stupids Die* (1985), and *The Stupids Take Off* (1989).

Adults find the humor in these books about a family too stupid to be believable. Would a father really wear socks as earmuffs? Would people wear clown suits to bed? But bringing their unbiased senses of humor to these hilarious books, children continue to laugh aloud at each crazy situation the unintelligent family members encounter.

Challenges

Removed from the Silver Star Elementary School in Vancouver, Washington (1985), because "it described families in a derogatory manner and might encourage children to disobey their parents."

Challenged at the Cunningham Elementary School in Beloit, Wisconsin (1985), because it "encourages disrespectful language."

Because the book makes parents look like "boobs" and undermines authority, the book was challenged, removed, and then returned to the shelves in the Horsham, Pennsylvania, schools, in 1993.

Reviews

Booklist 70 (July 15, 1974): 1251.

Bulletin of the Center for Children's Books 28 (Nov. 1974): 37.

Kirkus Reviews 42 (April 1, 1974): 359.

Library Journal 99 (April 15, 1974): 1210.

Publishers Weekly 205 (April 22, 1974): 74.

Articles about This Book

Tisdale, Sallie. "The Real Happy Ending." *Utne Reader* 25 (Jan./Feb. 1988): 114–17.

Background

Marcus, Leonard. "PW Interviews." (J. Marshall) *Publishers Weekly* 236 (July 28, 1989): 202–3.

Awards and Prizes

Library Journal's Best Books for Spring, 1974

Children's Book Showcase, 1975

School Library Journal's Best of the Best, 1966–1978

References about the Author

Contemporary Authors. Detroit: Gale, 1985. v. 113, pp. 20–23.

Contemporary Authors, New Revision Series. Detroit: Gale, 1993. v. 38, pp. 15–17.

Something about the Author. Detroit: Gale, 1986. v. 42, pp. 23–28.

Sources Recommending This Book

Gillespie, John T. *The Elementary School Paperback Collection.* Chicago: American Library Association, 1985.

Gillespie, John T., and Christine Gilbert, eds. *Best Books for Children: Preschool through the Middle Grades.* 3rd ed. New York: R. R. Bowker, 1985.

Lee, Lauren K., ed. *The Elementary School Library Collection: A Guide to Books and Other Media.* 18th ed. Williamsport, Pa.: Brodart, 1992.

The Indian in the Cupboard

New York: Doubleday, 1981

It's Omri's birthday and he receives three interesting presents: a used, plastic toy Indian from his best friend, Patrick; a medicine cabinet, found in an alley, given to him by his older brother; and some old used keys from his mother, one of which happens to fit the medicine cabinet. Much to his surprise, these secondhand presents turn out to be the most memorable of his life.

Omri, excited to use his new cabinet, locks the toy Indian inside. He is awakened the next morning by noise coming from inside the cabinet. Terrified, he slowly opens the cabinet, and standing inside, ready for attack, is the now alive Indian!

Patrick, feeling guilty for giving Omri a used toy, buys him a plastic cowboy, to go with the plastic Indian. Once the Indian comes to life, Omri discovers he is quite demanding. Omri provides food, shelter, and protection, but the Indian wants more. He wants a horse, a wife, and to be chief.

As the Indian and the cowboy are depicted as distinct individuals, this tale of children in imaginative play escalates to a logical ending. Omri, eventually, learns there is something inherently wrong with manipulating toys and friends.

This novel was recently made into a major motion picture.

Challenges

Because this book, along with *Return of the Indian*, also by Banks, was said to contain subtle stereotypes inconsistent with district diversity goals, the two books were removed, by the Bemijdi, Minnesota, School Board, from the school's voluntary reading list and from school library shelves, in 1995.

In 1993, the school librarian at the Suwannee County, Florida, Elementary School routinely erased words deemed objectionable from books. In this instance, the words "heck" and "hell" were removed.

Reviews

Bulletin of the Center for Children's Books 35 (Oct. 1981): 22.

Horn Book 57 (Dec. 1981): 662.

Publishers Weekly 220 (Oct. 16, 1981): 79.

School Library Journal 28 (Dec. 1981): 59.

Background

Children's Literature Review. Detroit: Gale, 1991. v. 24, pp. 186–200.

Contemporary Literary Criticism. Detroit: Gale, 1983. v. 23, pp. 40–43.

Something about the Author. Detroit: Gale, 1994. v. 75, pp. 153–56; v. 22, pp. 208–9.

Sources Recommending This Book

Children's Catalog. 16th ed. Juliette Yaakov. New York: H. W. Wilson, 1991.

Colborn, Candy. *What Do Children Read Next? A Reader's Guide to Fiction for Children.* Detroit: Gale, 1994.

Freeman, Judy. *Books Kids Will Sit Still For: The Complete Read-Aloud Guide.* 2nd ed. New York: R. R. Bowker, 1990.

Gillespie, John T. *The Elementary School Paperback Collection.* Chicago: American Library Association, 1985.

Gillespie, John T., and Christine Gilbert, eds. *Best Books for Children: Preschool through the Middle Grades.* 3rd ed. New York: R. R. Bowker, 1985.

Lee, Lauren K., ed. *The Elementary School Library Collection: A Guide to Books and Other Media.* 18th ed. Williamsport, Pa.: Brodart, 1992.

Mockett, Sara, and Ann Welton. "Fiction for the Gifted." *Booklist* 88 (Sept. 1, 1991): 66–67.

Blubber

New York: Dell Publishing, 1974

In this tale of peer pressure among suburban, well-to-do classmates, written by acclaimed author Judy Blume, Jill Brenner goes along when her classmates make fun of an overweight classmate, Linda Fischer. Linda presents an oral report about whales and the uses of their blubber. Wendy, the group's ringleader, nicknames Linda "Blubber."

Linda's report on whales gives Jill an idea for a Halloween costume, a flenser (one who strips blubber off whales). After Jill does not win the contest, Jill and her best friend, Tracy, go trick-or-treating armed with rotten eggs, silly string, and toilet paper. They break eggs into the mailbox of Mr. Machinist, and to prove it to Wendy, return to the scene, where Mr. Machinist is waiting with a camera.

As Jill's classmates continue to entertain themselves with lists of "how to have fun with Blubber," Mr. Machinist shows the families in the neighborhood the pictures he took Halloween night in order to identify the guilty parties. Jill and Tracy are caught and must admit they are sorry and rake leaves for Mr. Machinist.

To prove who told on Jill and Tracy, a mock trial is planned. When Linda isn't given a lawyer, Jill tells Wendy off and becomes the odd one out. Jill realizes she was acting mean not because she is mean, but because of the pressure of fitting in. Jill never learns that it is wrong to persecute someone; she simply learns that once the tables are turned, it hurts.

In its review, the *Bulletin of the Center for Children's Books* wrote, "A good family story as well as a school story, this had good characterization and dialogue, a vigorous first-person writing style, and—Judy Blume demonstrates again—a respectful and perceptive understanding of the anguished concerns of the pre-teen years."

Challenges

Because in the book, "bad is never punished. Good never comes to the fore. Evil is triumphant," the book was challenged at the Perry Township, Ohio, elementary school libraries in 1991.

Challenged, but retained, in the Bozeman, Montana, school libraries (1985) because the book was deemed profane, immoral, and offensive.

Challenged at the Muskego, Wisconsin, Elementary School (1986) because "the characters curse and the leader of the taunting (of an overweight girl) is never punished for her cruelty."

Restricted at the Lindenwold, New Jersey, elementary school libraries (1984) because of "a problem with language."

Because of its strong sexual content and language, and alleged lack of social or literary value, the book was banned but later restricted to students with parental permission at the Peoria, Illinois, School District libraries, in 1984.

Removed from the Hanover, Pennsylvania, School District's elementary and secondary libraries (1984) but later placed on a "restricted shelf" at middle-school libraries because the book was "indecent and inappropriate."

Reviews

Booklist 71 (Jan. 1, 1975): 459.

Bulletin of the Center for Children's Books 28 (May 1975): 142.

Kirkus Reviews 42 (Oct. 1, 1974): 1059.

Publishers Weekly 206 (Nov. 25, 1974): 45.

Reading Teacher 29 (Jan. 1976): 421.

School Librarian 28 (June 1980): 147.

School Library Journal 21 (Nov. 1974): 54.

Teacher 92 (March 1975): 112.

Background

Blume, Judy. *Letters to Judy: What Your Kids Wish They Could Tell You.* New York: Putnam, 1986.

Blume, Judy. "Tales of a Mother/Con-

fessor." *Newsweek* 115 (Summer/ Fall 1990): 18.

Bohning, Patricia, and Ann Keith Nauman. "Judy Blume: The Lady and the Legend." (bibliographical essay) *Emergency Librarian* 14 (Nov./Dec. 1986): 17–20.

"Censorship in Children's Books." (symposium) *Publishers Weekly* 232 (July 24, 1987): 108–11.

Merrill, Martha. "It's Still Judy Blume: Censorship in Alabama." (Alabama Library Association IFC survey) *Southeastern Librarian* 40 (Winter 1990): 168–69.

Moe, Laura. "Who's Afraid of Judy Blume?" (why book banners target works of fiction; bibliographical essay) *Book Report* 11 (March/April 1993): 21.

Rice, Susan J. "I've Bought All the Judy Blume—Now What Do I Do? Book Selection for Young Adults." *Ohio Library Association Bulletin* 56 (April 1986): 22–24.

Awards and Prizes

Arizona Young Readers Award, 1977

North Dakota Children's Choice Award, 1983

Young Readers Choice Award, Pacific Northwest Library Association, 1977

References about the Author

Children's Literature Review. Detroit: Gale, 1976. v. 2, pp. 15–19.

Contemporary Authors. Detroit: Gale, 1978. v. 29–32, p. 72.

Contemporary Authors, New Revision Series. Detroit: Gale, 1992. v. 37. pp. 42–47; v. 13, pp. 59–62.

Contemporary Literary Criticism. Detroit: Gale, 1980. v. 30, p. 47.

Dictionary of Literary Biography. Detroit: Gale, 1986. v. 52, pp. 30–38.

Something about the Author. Detroit: Gale, 1995. v. 79, pp. 20–26; v. 31, pp. 28–34; v. 2, pp. 31–32.

Sources Recommending This Book

Colborn, Candy. *What Do Children Read Next? A Reader's Guide to Fiction for Children.* Detroit: Gale, 1994.

Gillespie, John T. *The Elementary School Paperback Collection.* Chicago: American Library Association, 1985.

Gillespie, John T. *The Junior High School Paperback Collection.* Chicago: American Library Association, 1985.

Gillespie, John T., and Christine Gilbert, eds. *Best Books for Children: Preschool through the Middle Grades.* 3rd ed. New York: R. R. Bowker, 1985.

Lee, Lauren K., ed. *The Elementary School Library Collection: A Guide to Books and Other Media.* 18th ed. Williamsport, Pa.: Brodart, 1992.

The Young Adult Reader's Adviser: The Best in Literature and Language Arts, Mathematics and Computer Science. Vol. 1. Ed. Myra Immell. New Providence, N.J.: R. R. Bowker, 1992.

The Goats

New York: Farrar, Straus, Giroux, 1987

At summer camp, Laura and Howie, who are social outcasts, are taken to a deserted island, stripped, and abandoned. Fearing further ridicule, they use a floating log to return to the mainland; break into a locked summer cabin where they find food, clothes, and warmth; and call Laura's mother, asking her to come and take them away from this despicable situation. As a result of a major breakdown in communication between the two, Laura's mother insists that Laura stay at camp and try to adjust to the situation. Not wanting to return and face their horrid camp-mates, Laura and Howie run away. In order to survive this physically and emotionally draining ordeal, they become burglars but do plan to pay everyone back for damages incurred. In their flight from the camp, the twosome encounters a group of youngsters from another camp who befriend them; a suspicious hotel cleaning lady who accuses them of indecent behavior; a kind, old man who lends them money; and a mean, unpleasant deputy sheriff who finally arrests them.

This captivating novel explores many complex themes. A seemingly senseless but cruel prank has severe and far-reaching consequences on the lives of Howie, Laura, and her mother, Maddy. Howie and Laura experience extreme alienation from loved ones, peers, and other adults. Because they believe that they only have each other, they begin to depend on each other and gradually gain each other's trust. As their intense relationship grows, Howie and Laura gain inner strength and feelings of self-confidence. By the end of the powerful, compelling novel, they have emotionally grown in many positive ways, which enable them to move forward and overcome their status of goats—social outcasts.

Maddy, Laura's mother, also gains much emotional insight because of the incident. She realizes that she hasn't been the mother that Laura deserves and that she definitely didn't handle the incident in the best way possible. Overall, her newly found concern for Laura's well-being and love for her daughter are evident at the novel's end.

This novel, written by an acclaimed writer and illustrator of picture books, was praised by many professional reviewers. *Horn Book* stated, "This novel by a welcome new voice promises to become a significant addition to the body of children's literature."

Booklist added, "Its many layers of concern, its relativity to today, its strength as a piece of writing, and its appeal for children mark this novel as one that will leave lingering echoes in readers' minds long after the story is over."

Anita Silvey, in an article that appeared in *Horn Book,* discussed the negative criticism. She wrote, "Critics of the book are concerned with the absence of positive adult characters—as was the case with *Harriet the Spy*—and the change in the young protagonists from innocents to thieves. And all adult readers, I think, are disturbed by the raw emotion in the book—and the feelings brought forth from the reader."

Challenges

Because it contains a passage describing the rescue of a naked girl, the book was removed from the Housel Middle School library in Prosser, Washington, in 1992.

Challenged at the Timberland Regional Middle School in Plaistow, New Hampshire (1994), because parents said it contained "offensive and inappropriate" language for seventh-graders.

Reviews

Booklist 84 (Nov. 15, 1987): 564.

Bulletin of the Center for Children's Books 41 (Oct. 1987): 24.

Horn Book 64 (Jan. 1988): 68.

Kliatt Young Adult Paperback Book Guide 24 (Sept. 1990): 6.

New York Times Book Review 92 (Nov. 8, 1987): 31.

Publishers Weekly 237 (Jan. 1990): 112.

School Library Journal 34 (Nov. 1987): 113.

Voice of Youth Advocates 11 (April 1988): 22.

Articles about This Book

Campbell, Patty. "The Young Adult Perplex." *Wilson Library Bulletin* 62 (Jan. 1988): 75–76.

Silvey, Anita. "Editorial: *The Goats.*" *Horn Book* 64 (Jan. 1988): 23.

Background

Endicott, Alba Quinones. "Females Also Come of Age." *English Journal* 81 (April 1992): 42–47.

McDonnell, Christine. "New Voices, New Visions: Brock Cole." *Horn Book* 65 (Sept./Oct. 1989): 602–5.

Rochman, Hazel. "The YA Connection: *Celine:* A Talk with the Author." (Brock Cole) *Booklist* 86 (Oct. 15, 1989): 441–42.

Rochman, Hazel. "The YA Connection: *Celine,* Brock Cole, and Holden Caulfield." (significant new YA novel in the tradition of Salinger) *Booklist* 86 (Oct. 15, 1989): 440.

Awards and Prizes

Best Books for Young Adults, 1987

New York Times Notable Book, 1987

Notable Children's Book, 1987

References about the Author

Children's Literature Review. Detroit: Gale, 1989. v. 18, pp. 81–85.

Contemporary Authors. Detroit: Gale, 1992. v. 136, pp. 84–86.

Something about the Author. Detroit: Gale, 1993. v. 72, pp. 34–38.

Sources Recommending This Book

Carter, Betty, comp. "Teaching through Literature." *Booklist* 86 (May 1, 1990): 1696.

Children's Catalog. 16th ed. Ed. Juliette Yaakov. New York: H. W. Wilson, 1991.

Donavin, Denise Perry. *Best of the Best for Children.* Chicago: American Library Association, 1992.

Estes, Sally, ed. *Genre Favorites for Young Adults.* Chicago: American Library Association, 1993.

Estes, Sally, ed. *Growing Up Is Hard to Do.* Chicago: American Library Association, 1994.

Gillespie, John T., ed. *Best Books for Junior High Readers.* New Providence, N.J.: R. R. Bowker, 1991.

Gillespie, John T., and Corinne J. Naden. eds. *Best Books for Children: Preschool through Grade Six.* New Providence, N.J.: R. R. Bowker, 1994.

Junior High School Library Catalog. 16th ed. Ed. Juliette Yaakov. New York: H. W. Wilson, 1990.

Rochman, Hazel. *Against Borders: Promoting Books for a Multicultural World.* Chicago: American Library Association, 1993.

Scales, Pat, comp. "Children's Novels to Teach." *Booklist* 85 (Feb. 1, 1989): 944.

Zvirin, Stephanie. *The Best Years of Their Lives: A Resource Guide for Teenagers in Crisis.* Chicago: American Library Association, 1992.

JAMES LINCOLN COLLIER and CHRISTOPHER COLLIER

My Brother Sam Is Dead

New York: Four Winds Press, 1974

Based upon actual events, *My Brother Sam Is Dead* tells the story of the Meeker family during the American Revolution. The story is told through the eyes of thirteen-year-old Tim, whose sixteen-year-old brother, Sam, leaves Yale to join the Continental army. Tim and Sam's father is a marginal loyalist who doesn't want to see a war. Although Tim witnesses the conflict in his family when his brother joins Benedict Arnold's regiment, the war still seems far away. The reality of war becomes too real for Tim when he and his father make the annual trip to sell their cattle. It is the first time Tim has been allowed to accompany his father on the usually routine trip, and it opens his eyes to a new world. On the return trip, however, Tim's father is taken prisoner for selling beef that will feed British troops. When his father eventually dies on a British prison ship (the family is unsure how he has come to be on a British ship), Tim is left to run the family's tavern with his mother, who begins to sink into depression. Seeing his neighbors killed by British troops and his brother unjustly accused and executed as a cattle thief by the Continental army keeps Tim from getting involved in the war. Years later, when he is in his sixties, Tim reflects upon the war and wonders if there may have been another way to gain independence.

My Brother Sam Is Dead is a realistic depiction of the horrors of war and its effect on civilians. The authors vividly depict Tim's world—James Lincoln Collier is a professional writer and Christopher Collier is a professor of early American history—while using modern dialect, because "nobody is really sure how people talked in those days."

Because this is a book about war, the situations are complicated and there are no easy answers. The characters are complex, with no clear heroes or villains. Sam is idealistic and wants to do what he thinks is right, yet he disobeys his father, which Tim knows is a sin. Tim's neighbors are both rebels and Tories, but he does not take sides; nor is he able to accept death on either side. While it is not an easy book, it is one that vividly portrays the Revolutionary era and the horrors of war.

The *Bulletin of the Center for Children's Books* wrote, "Well-paced, the story blends fact and fiction adroitly; the characterization is solid and the writing convincingly that of a young boy concerned more with his own problems and family in wartime than with issues or principles."

Challenges

Due to profanity and violence, challenged, but retained, at the Palmyra, Pennsylvania, area schools, in 1994.

Removed from fifth-grade classes at Bryant Ranch Elementary School in the Placentia-Yorba Linda, California, Unified School District (1994) because "the book is not G-rated. Offensive language is offensive language. Graphic violence is graphic violence, no matter what the context."

Challenged at the Walnut Elementary School in Emporia, Kansas (1993), by parents who said that it contained profanity and graphic violence.

Because the book uses the names of God and Jesus in a "vain and profane manner along with inappropriate sexual references," the book was challenged in the Greenville County, South Carolina, schools, in 1991.

Removed from the curriculum of fifth-grade classes in New Richmond, Ohio (1989), because the book contains the words "bastard," "goddamn," and "hell" and did not represent "acceptable ethical standards for fifth graders."

Reviews

Booklist 71 (Oct. 15, 1974): 241.

Bulletin of the Center for Children's Books 28 (March 1975): 108.

Horn Book 51 (April 1975): 152.

Library Journal 99 (Dec. 15, 1974): 3271.

Publishers Weekly 206 (Nov. 25, 1974): 45.

Awards and Prizes

American Book Award nomination, 1975

Jane Addams Peace Prize, 1975

National Book Award finalist, 1975

Newbery Medal Award Honor Book, 1975

Notable Children's Book, 1975

References about the Author

Children's Literature Review. Detroit: Gale, 1978. v. 3, pp. 44–49.

Contemporary Authors. Detroit: Gale, 1974. v. 9–12, p. 179.

Contemporary Authors, New Revision Series. Detroit: Gale, 1991. v. 33, pp. 92–94; v. 4, pp. 149–50.

Contemporary Literary Criticism. Detroit: Gale, 1984. v. 30, pp. 71–75.

Something about the Author. Detroit: Gale, 1993. v. 70, pp. 39–43; v. 8, pp. 33–34.

Sources Recommending This Book

Children's Catalog. 16th ed. Ed. Juliette Yaakov. New York: H. W. Wilson, 1991.

Colborn, Candy. *What Do Children Read Next? A Reader's Guide to Fiction for Children.* Detroit: Gale, 1994.

Cooper, Ilene, comp. "Past and Perilous: Historical Adventures." *Booklist* 86 (Jan. 1, 1990): 923–24.

Donavin, Denise Perry. *Best of the Best for Children.* Chicago: American Library Association, 1992.

Elleman, Barbara, and Ginny Moore Kruse, comps. "Contemporary Issues—Peace." *Booklist* 83 (April 15, 1987): 1299–1301.

Freeman, Judy. *Books Kids Will Sit Still For: The Complete Read-Aloud Guide.* 2nd ed. New York: R. R. Bowker, 1990.

Gillespie, John T., ed. *Best Books for Junior High Readers.* New Providence, N.J.: R. R. Bowker, 1991.

Gillespie, John T. *The Elementary School Paperback Collection.* Chicago: American Library Association, 1985.

Gillespie, John T. *The Junior High School Paperback Collection.* Chicago: American Library Association, 1985.

Gillespie, John T., and Christine Gilbert, eds. *Best Books for Children: Preschool through the Middle Grades.* 3rd ed. New York: R. R. Bowker, 1985.

Junior High School Library Catalog. 16th ed. Ed. Juliette Yaakov. New York: H. W. Wilson, 1990.

Lee, Lauren K., ed. *The Elementary School Library Collection: A Guide to Books and Other Media.* 18th ed. Williamsport, Pa.: Brodart, 1992.

Middle and Junior High School Library Catalog. 7th ed. Ed. Ann Price and Juliette Yaakov. New York: H. W. Wilson, 1995.

"More Novels to Teach." *Booklist* 86 (March 1, 1990): 1354–55.

Shapiro, Lillian L., ed. *Fiction for Youth: A Guide to Recommended Books.* 2nd ed. New York: Neal-Schuman Publishers, 1986.

Weber, Rosemary. "Building a Children's Literature Collection: A Suggested Basic Collection of Children's Books, 1975 Supplement." *Choice* 12 (Nov. 1975): 1123–32.

The Young Adult Reader's Adviser: The Best in Social Sciences, History, Science and Health. Vol. 2. Ed. Myra Immell. New Providence, N.J.: R. R. Bowker, 1992.

James and the Giant Peach

New York: Knopf, 1961

When James Henry Trotter's parents get eaten by an angry rhinoceros that has escaped from the London Zoo, he goes to live on top of a hill with his only living relatives—two mean, horrid aunts. James is expected to do all the chores around the house. He cannot play with other children.
The aunts call him names, beat him, and deny him food. And he is constantly punished for acting just like a child. But in spite of his abhorrent existence, James remains cheerful and optimistic about life and all that it has to offer him.

One day, the first of many peculiar things happens to James. He meets an old man who gives him a bag of magical and powerful tiny green things. In his excitement, James trips and falls, spilling the bag's contents all over the ground.

These green things cause a giant peach to grow on a usually barren peach tree. And much to James's surprise, five life-size, talking insects live inside the peach. James joins Miss Spider, Ladybug, Old-Green-Grasshopper, Earthworm, and Centipede in a marvelous, exciting journey as the giant peach and its inhabitants travel by land, sea, and air to New York.

This whimsical, clever fantasy includes vivid scenes of death—James's parents getting eaten by a rhinoceros and his awful aunts getting squashed by the giant peach—use of language that kids have always delighted in, and the awful neglect James suffers while living with his dreadful aunts.

The novel's final message is positive. James experienced many hardships and coped with many difficult situations, but in the end, he overcomes them all and has a rich, successful life, as do his traveling companions.

Challenges

Challenged at the Deep Creek Elementary School, in Charlotte Harbor, Florida (1991), because it is "not appropriate reading material for young children."

Because the book uses the word "ass" and parts of the book deal with wine, tobacco, and snuff, the book was challenged at the Peterson Elementary School, in Altoona, Wisconsin, in 1991.

Challenged at the Morton Elementary School Library, in Brooksville, Florida (1992), because the book contains a foul word and promotes drugs and whiskey.

Background

"Censorship in Children's Books" (symposium). *Publishers Weekly* 232 (July 24, 1987): 108–11.

Columbo, Cristina. "Roald Dahl." (violence in children's literature) *Bookbird* 31 (Sept. 1993): 27.

Hitchens, Christopher. "The Grimmest Tales." *Vanity Fair* 57 (Jan. 1994): 26–30.

Tisdale, Sallie. "The Real Happy Ending." *Utne Reader* 25 (Jan./Feb. 1988): 114–17.

References about the Author

Children's Literature Review. Detroit: Gale, 1984. v. 7, pp. 63–84; v. 1, pp. 49–52.

Contemporary Authors, New Revision Series. Detroit: Gale, 1992. v. 37, pp. 123–28; v. 32, pp. 107–9; v. 6, pp. 119–21.

Contemporary Literary Criticism. Detroit: Gale, 1994. v. 79, pp. 177–182.

Something about the Author. Detroit: Gale, 1993. v. 73, pp. 39–46; v. 26, pp. 50–61; v. 1, p. 74.

Sources Recommending This Book

Children's Catalog. 16th ed. Ed. Juliette Yaakov. New York: H. W. Wilson, 1991.

Colborn, Candy. *What Do Children Read Next? A Reader's Guide to Fiction for Children.* Detroit: Gale, 1994.

Freeman, Judy. *Books Kids Will Sit Still For: The Complete Read-Aloud Guide.* 2nd ed. New York: R. R. Bowker, 1990.

Gillespie, John T. *The Elementary School Paperback Collection.* Chicago: American Library Association, 1985.

Gillespie, John T., and Christine Gilbert, eds. *Best Books for Children: Preschool through the Middle Grades.* 3rd ed. New York: R. R. Bowker, 1985.

Lee, Lauren K., ed. *The Elementary School Library Collection: A Guide to Books and Other Media.* 18th ed. Williamsport, Pa.: Brodart, 1992.

A Wrinkle in Time

New York: Farrar, Straus and Giroux, 1962

Mr. Murry, who suddenly disappeared while working for the government on a tesseract* project, has been gone for a year. His wife and four children, Meg, Charles Wallace, and the twins, Sandy and Dennys, are extremely worried about their father's life and his whereabouts. Late one stormy night, Meg, Charles Wallace, and their mother are in the kitchen drinking hot chocolate, when a strange old lady, Mrs. Whatsit, comes to visit. She warns them that Mr. Murry is in extreme danger and that she and her two friends have come to help save him. Knowing that only they can save their father from the Dark Thing, Meg and Charles Wallace, with the help of their new friend, Calvin O'Keefe, and the three odd women, tesseract through time and space to find Mr. Murry and fight for his life.

Using powerful forces, the group tesseracts to other galaxies and planets in far distant times to accomplish their mission—save Mr. Murry. Throughout this harrowing journey, the traveling companions encounter many dreadful creatures and experience many frightening situations. Although Charles Wallace and Calvin are brave, Meg, in an act of courage and love, endangers her own life by tesseracting back to the place where Charles Wallace has accidently been left behind. She saves Charles Wallace, proving that love does triumph over evil.

Published in 1962, this novel was one of the first to portray women as positive role models for young readers. Mrs. Murry is a scientist, certainly not a typical career for a mother in the sixties; and the main protagonist, Meg, is the true heroine in this powerful novel of the desperate struggle between good and evil. Meg is one of just a few female main characters in science fiction books for children that were being published at the time. Over the past decades, these two female characters have remained strong role models for young girls throughout the country.

Using tidbits of information from the disciplines of religion, science, and philosophy and combining them with satire, and allegory, L'Engle has written a sometimes confusing but dramatic, compelling science-fiction novel. This winner of the 1963 Newbery Medal Award remains popular fare for sci-fi fans.

---

*Tesseract (verb): To travel the shortest distance between two points, not by moving in a straight line but by a fold or wrinkle.

Challenges

Because the book sends a mixed signal to children about good and evil, the book was challenged in the Anniston, Alabama, schools in 1990. The complainant also objected to listing the name of Jesus Christ together with the names of great artists, philosophers, scientists, and religious leaders when referring to defenders of Earth against evil.

Challenged, but retained, on the media-center shelves of the Polk City, Florida, Elementary School in 1985.

Reviews

Booklist 58 (April 1, 1962): 535.

Horn Book 38 (April 1962): 177.

Library Journal 87 (March 15, 1962): 1332.

Wilson Library Bulletin 58 (May 1962): 182.

Background

Dohner, Jan. "Literature of Change: Science Fiction and Women." *Top of the News* (Spring 1978): 261–65.

Gonzales, Doreen. *Madeleine L'Engle: Author of A Wrinkle in Time.* New York: Dillon Press, 1991.

Jones, Raymond E. *A Literature Guide to A Wrinkle in Time.* Cambridge, Mass.: Book Wise, 1991.

Rakow, Susan R. "Young-Adult Literature for Honors Students?" *English Journal* 80 (Jan. 1991): 48–51.

Awards and Prizes

Hans Christian Andersen Award runner-up, 1964

Lewis Carroll Shelf Award, 1965

Newbery Medal Award, 1963

Sequoyah Children's Book Award, from the Oklahoma State Department of Education, 1965

References about the Author

Children's Literature Review. Detroit: Gale, 1988. v. 14, pp. 132–56; v. 1, pp. 129–34.

Contemporary Authors. Detroit: Gale, 1967. v. 1–4, pp. 582–83.

Contemporary Authors, New Revision Series. Detroit: Gale, 1992. v. 39, pp. 226–30; v. 21, pp. 240–43; v. 3, pp. 331–32.

Contemporary Literary Criticism. Detroit: Gale, 1980. v. 12, pp. 346–52.

Dictionary of Literary Biography. Detroit: Gale, 1986. v. 52, pp. 241–49.

Something about the Author. Detroit: Gale, 1994. v. 75, pp. 114–21; v. 27, pp. 131–40; v. 1, pp. 141–42.

Sources Recommending This Book

"Becoming a Lifetime Reader." *Book Links* 87 (Jan. 15, 1991): 1018–21

Children's Catalog. 16th ed. Ed. Juliette Yaakov. New York: H. W. Wilson, 1991.

Eaken, Mary K., comp. *Good Books for Children: A Selection of Outstanding Children's Books Published 1950–1965.* Chicago: University of Chicago Press, 1966.

Estes, Sally, ed. *Growing Up Is Hard to Do.* Chicago: American Library Association, 1994.

Freeman, Judy. *Books Kids Will Sit Still For: The Complete Read-Aloud Guide.* 2nd ed. New York: R. R. Bowker, 1990.

Gillespie, John T., ed. *Best Books for Junior High Readers.* New Providence, N.J.: R. R. Bowker, 1991.

Gillespie, John T. *The Elementary School Paperback Collection.* Chicago: American Library Association, 1985.

Gillespie, John T. *The Junior High School Paperback Collection.* Chicago: American Library Association, 1985.

Gillespie, John T., and Christine Gilbert, eds. *Best Books for Children: Preschool through the Middle Grades.* 3rd ed. New York: R. R. Bowker, 1985.

Junior High School Library Catalog. 16th ed. Ed. Juliette Yaakov. New York: H. W. Wilson, 1990.

Lee, Lauren K., ed. *The Elementary School Library Collection: A Guide to Books and Other Media.* 18th ed. Williamsport, Pa.: Brodart, 1992.

Middle and Junior High School Library Catalog. 7th ed. Ed. Ann Price and Juliette Yaakov. New York: H. W. Wilson, 1995.

Miller, Frances A. "Books to Read When You Hate to Read." *Booklist* 88 (Feb. 15, 1992): 1101.

Mockett, Sara, and Ann Weltori. "Fiction for the Gifted." *Booklist* 88 (Sept. 1, 1991): 66–67.

"See How They Grow." *Children's Literature in Education* 18 (Spring 1987): 37.

"Still Good Reading: Adolescent Novels Written before 1967." *English Journal* 81 (April 1992): 90.

The Giver

New York: Houghton Mifflin, 1993

This Newbery Medal Award–winning book, written by acclaimed children's author Lois Lowry, tells the story of Jonas as he reaches his twelfth year—when he will become a Twelve and receive his life assignment. Jonas and his family, which includes his parents and his sister, Lily, who is a Six, live in a community that has adopted Sameness. Sameness means their lives are carefully structured by the community; none of the members has to make his or her own decisions or choices—the community takes care of everything.

Jonas's protected life is shattered when he learns that his life assignment is to be that of Receiver of Memory—the one person in the community who maintains memories of the time before Sameness. When Jonas begins his training with the former Receiver, who is now known as the Giver, he receives pleasant memories—sunsets, sailing, holidays, sunshine, and color—that existed before Sameness. Eventually, he is forced to experience unpleasant emotions—sadness, loneliness, and pain. Jonas is forbidden to discuss what he has learned with other members of the community, who remain protected from emotions and pain. Jonas's isolation grows as he begins to experience what his family and friends will never understand—music, love, colors.

Jonas is forced to make a decision when he learns that Gabriel—a baby whom the family has been caring for—is to be "released" for failing to thrive. Before becoming the Receiver, Jonas thought that being released merely meant going to another place—the mythical Elsewhere—but he learns that release actually means death. To make matters worse, Jonas's father, who is a Nurturer, is assigned to do the release. With the blessings of the Giver, Jonas takes the baby and sets off on his bike in search of Elsewhere.

The Giver presents complicated issues—euthanasia, conformity in a cultlike society, and the suppression of personal freedom, among others. By identifying with Jonas, however, readers are clearly aware of the problems of this society. Lowry may not provide readers with a happy ending, but neither does she give us easy answers.

Horn Book wrote, "The story is skillfully written; the air of disquiet is delicately insinuated. And the theme of balancing the values of freedom and security is beautifully presented."

Challenges

The book, along with short stories by James Baldwin, Sam Keith, Kurt

Vonnegut Jr., and Don Wulfson, was challenged but retained by a unanimous vote, as part of the Elk Grove, California, Unified School District's curriculum, in 1995.

Temporarily banned from classes by the Bonita Unified School District, in La Verne and San Dimas, California (1994), after four parents complained that violent and sexual passages were inappropriate for children.

Reviews

Booklist 89 (April 15, 1993): 1506.

Bulletin of the Center for Children's Books 46 (April 1993): 257.

Horn Book 69 (July 1993): 458.

Publishers Weekly 240 (Feb. 15, 1993): 240.

School Library Journal 39 (May 1993): 124.

Voice of Youth Advocates 16 (Aug. 1993): 167.

Wilson Library Bulletin 68 (Oct. 1993): 122.

Articles about This Book

Campbell, Patty. "The Sand in the Oyster." *Horn Book* 69 (Nov./Dec. 1993): 717–21.

Lowry, Lois. "1994 Newbery Acceptance Speech." *Journal of Youth Services in Libraries* 7 (Summer 1994): 361–67.

Silvey, Anita. "*The Giver*." (Lois Lowry's new book and risk taking in children's literature) *Horn Book* 69 (July/Aug. 1993): 392.

"The Gift of Memory." (using Lois Lowry's *The Giver* with grades 7–12) *School Librarian's Workshop* 14 (April 1994): 8–9.

Walters, Karla. "Other voices: Pills against Sexual 'Stirrings' in Lowry's *The Giver*." *Bookbird* 32 (Summer 1994): 35–36.

Background

Haley-James, Shirley. "Lois Lowry." *Horn Book* 66 (July/Aug. 1990): 422–24.

Lorraine, Walter. "Lois Lowry." *Horn Book* 70 (July/Aug. 1994): 423–26.

Smith, Amanda. "PW Interviews: Lois Lowry." (writer of young adults' books) *Publishers Weekly* 229 (Feb. 21, 1986): 152–53.

Woolf, Vera, Patricia Conover, and Alice Resnick. "Focus On: Lois Lowry." (discussion and writing activities) *School Librarian's Workshop* 12 (April 1992): 6–7.

Awards and Prizes

Newbery Medal Award, 1994

Halloween ABC

New York: Macmillan, 1987

Written by one of the best contemporary poets for children, this collection of 26 inventive, original poems evokes the spooky, eerie feel of the Halloween season. The picture book format is deceptive, because this collection is definitely not for preschoolers who are learning the alphabet. The sophisticated subject matter and sinister illustrations are more appropriate for school-age children.

Some poems vividly describe elements of the darkness including bats, skeletons, fiends, ghosts, haunted houses, elves, and nightmares. Other poems describe horrid acts such as being murdered by a falling icicle or being nailed inside a coffin. Some poems are sinisterly scary in tone while others are ludicrously humorous. This combination of horror and humor adds to the genuine child appeal and continued popularity of the book.

Lane Smith, in his stellar debut as an illustrator, has painted dark, surrealistic paintings that perfectly complement the mood of the poems.

This attractively designed book explores the essences of Halloween and the epitome of wickedness that continually delight the dark side of children but regularly disturb parents.

Challenges

Because the book was believed to be too violent for children, it was challenged, but retained, in the Sandwich, Massachusetts, Public Library, in 1995.

Challenged in the Spokane, Washington, School District Library (1994) by a father who found the poems morbid and satanic. In particular, the parent disapproved of one poem that "appears to be a chant calling forth the devil."

Because the "poems promote Satanism, murder and suicide," the book was challenged, but retained, in the Cameron Elementary School Library in Rice Lake, Wisconsin, in 1993.

Challenged, but retained, at the Ennis, Texas, Public Library, in 1993.

Because the book "promotes violent criminal and deviant behavior," it was challenged, but retained, in the Othello, Washington, elementary school libraries, in 1993.

Challenged at the Howard County, Maryland, school libraries (1992) because "there should be an effort to tone down Halloween and there should not be books about it in the schools."

Challenged and retained, but will be shelved with other works generally available only to older students and won't be used in future Halloween displays at the Federal Way School District in Seattle, Washington, in 1992. The compromise was for a group of parents who objected to the book's satanic references.

Challenged at the Acres Green Elementary School in Douglas County, Colorado, in 1992.

Because it is "satanic and disgusting," the book was challenged in the Wichita, Kansas, public schools, in 1991.

Because the book allegedly encourages devil worshiping, the book was challenged at the Douglas County Library in Roseburg, Oregon, in 1989.

Reviews

Booklist 84 (Oct. 15, 1987): 398.

Bulletin of the Center for Children's Books 41 (Dec. 1987): 72.

Horn Book 63 (Nov. 1987): 753.

Publishers Weekly 232 (July 24, 1987): 186.

School Library Journal 34 (Nov. 1987): 100.

Articles about This Book

Hopkins, Lee Bennett, column editor. "Book Sharing: Poetry Update—1987." *School Library Media Quarterly* 16 (Spring 1988): 192.

Background

McHargue, Georgess. "A Ride across the Mystic Bridge or Occult Books: What, Why, and Who Needs Them?" In *Issues in Children's Book Selection: A School Library Journal/Library Journal Anthology.* New York: R. R. Bowker, 1973.

Awards and Prizes

New York Times Best Illustrated Award, 1987

References about the Author

Children's Literature Review. Detroit: Gale, 1988. v. 14, pp. 187–204.

Contemporary Authors. Detroit: Gale, 1969. v. 5–8, pp. 775–76.

Contemporary Authors, New Revision Series. Detroit: Gale, 1990. v. 137, p. 304; v. 29, pp. 295–99.

Something about the Author. Detroit: Gale, 1993. v. 73, pp. 153–59; v. 40, pp. 141–49; v. 3, pp. 128–29.

Sources Recommending This Book

Children's Catalog. 16th ed. Ed. Juliette Yaakov. New York: H. W. Wilson, 1991.

Ciancioli, Patricia J. *Picture Books for Children.* 3rd ed. Chicago: American Library Association, 1990.

Freeman, Judy. *More Books Kids Will Sit Still For.* New Providence, N.J.: R. R. Bowker, 1995.

Lee, Lauren K., ed. *The Elementary School Library Collection: A Guide to Books and Other Media.* 18th ed. Williamsport, Pa.: Brodart, 1992.

LESLEA NEWMAN

Heather Has Two Mommies

Northhampton, Mass.: In Other Words, 1989

This picture book tells the story of Heather, the daughter of a lesbian couple. The reader discovers how her parents met and decided to have a baby, and the story proceeds through Heather's early childhood to her enrollment in a preschool. It is at this point, in her interactions with the other children, that Heather learns her family is different because she does not have a father. The teacher asks the children to draw pictures of their families, revealing that each child has a different configuration of family members.

Heather Has Two Mommies is an exploration of the nature of families in general, while focusing on lesbian parents in particular.

The book is most successful when dealing with the question of family structure. It is interesting to see the preschool teacher illustrate to the children that every family is different in some way by having the children draw their family portraits. There is great warmth in this part of the book, and it is easy to see why Heather is comforted after the teacher hangs the pictures in the classroom. The book is least successful when discussing the mechanics of Heather's conception. The book, written for an audience of early elementary–age children, presupposes that its readers have a working knowledge of the reproductive process. Concepts such as "sperm and egg" and terms like "vagina" are used to describe to young readers the process of artificial insemination. All of this is clearly beyond the comprehension of most readers in the book's target audience.

Nevertheless, *Heather Has Two Mommies* provides validation of children in different family situations. For children of other kinds of families, the book shows that each family is special, which is important in a day when the family consisting of a mother, father, son, and daughter is no longer the norm.

Challenges

Challenged at the Chandler, Arizona, Public Library (1994) because the book is a "skillful presentation to the young child about lesbianism/homosexuality."

Removed by officials at the Lane County Head Start Center, in Cottage Grove, Oregon, in 1994.

Challenged, but retained, in the Oak Bluffs, Massachusetts, School Library, in 1994. Though the parent leading the protest stated that, "The subject matter . . . is obscene and vulgar and the message is that homosexuality is okay," the selection review committee voted unanimously to keep the book.

Challenged, but retained, at the Dayton and Montgomery County, Ohio, Public Library, in 1993.

Challenged at the Mesa, Arizona, Public Library (1993) because it "is vile, sick, and goes against every law and constitution."

Challenged at the North Brunswick, New Jersey, Public Library, in 1993.

Challenged at the Cumberland County, North Carolina, Public Library, in 1993.

Challenged at the Wicomico County Free Library, in Salisbury, Maryland, in 1993.

Moved from the children's section to the adult section at the Mercer County Library System, in Lawrence, New Jersey, in 1993.

Moved from the children's section to the adult section in an Elizabethtown, North Carolina, library (1993) because it "promotes a dangerous and ungodly lifestyle from which children must be protected."

Moved from the children's section to the young adult section at the Chestatee Regional Library System, in Gainesville, Georgia, in 1993. Three area legislators wanted the book removed and said, "We could put together a resolution to amend the Georgia state constitution to say that tax dollars cannot be used to promote homosexuality, pedophilia, or sadomasochism."

Because the school board objected to words that were "age inappropriate," the book was removed from the Brooklyn, New York, School District's curriculum, in 1992.

Challenged in Fayetteville, North Carolina, in 1992.

Reviews

Booklist 86 (March 1, 1990): 1354.

Bulletin of the Center for Children's Books 43 (Feb. 1990): 144.

Small Press Book Review 6 (July 1990): 20.

Articles about This Book

Loch, Marge Wouters. "Children's Cornucopia: Whose Family's Values? Gay and Lesbian Families in Children's Books." *WLW Journal* 15 (Winter 1992/1993): 13–14.

Background

Ford, Michael Thomas. "Gay Books for Young Readers: When Caution Calls the Shots." *Publishers Weekly* 241 (Feb. 21, 1994): 24–27.

References about the Author

Contemporary Authors. Detroit: Gale, 1989. v. 126, pp. 321–22.

Something about the Author. Detroit: Gale, 1993. v. 71, pp. 138–39.

KATHERINE PATERSON

Bridge to Terabithia

New York: HarperCollins, 1977

Jess Aarons is determined to become the best runner in his school; so determined is he that he practices daily over the summer in preparation. To his amazement, he is easily beaten in a race on the first day of school by a newcomer to the school and his new neighbor, Leslie Burke.

Although at first irritated with Leslie, Jess eventually becomes her friend and comes to appreciate the world Leslie comes from; a world he doesn't know that includes music, art, and culture. Leslie also uses her incredible imagination to create a secret kingdom in the woods, where the two of them rule, called Terabithia.

Their peaceful world is shattered one day when Jess is on a trip to Washington, D.C., and Leslie attempts to cross the rain-swollen river alone to Terabithia via a rope. The rope breaks and Leslie hits her head on a stone as she falls. After Leslie's death, Jess deals with myriad emotions—including those arising because his parents thought he was dead—that are thoughtfully and lovingly presented.

At the close of the story, Jess builds a bridge to Terabithia and takes his sister there safely.

In this Newbery Medal Award–winning book, Paterson weaves a tale of friendship and tragedy. This novel permeates the thoughts and feelings of children and adults alike. Jess's parents, who never showed much emotion, are remarkably understanding after Leslie's death. Mrs. Myers, a teacher at Jess and Leslie's school and somewhat of a tyrant, also needs consoling.

Jack Forman, reviewing for *School Library Journal,* wrote, "Jess and Leslie are so effectively developed as characters that young readers might well feel that they were their classmates." The reviewer in the *Bulletin of the Center for Children's Books* writes, "Quite unlike Paterson's previous books in setting or theme, this is just as beautifully crafted and convincing, but even more touching."

Public Media Video produced a movie based on the book as part of their Wonderworks series. The movie won an American Film and Video Festival Blue Ribbon in 1992.

Challenges

In 1995, a group of parents asked the Medway, Maine, School Board to stop fifth-grade students from reading two books in class. The parents charged that *The Castle in the Attic,* by Elizabeth Winthrop, and *Bridge to*

Terabithia use swear words and deal with sorcery.

Challenged in the Gettysburg, Pennsylvania, public schools (1993) because of offensive language.

In 1993, a challenge to this book in Oskaloosa, Kansas, led to the enactment of a new policy that requires teachers to examine their required material for profanities. Teachers will list each profanity and the number of times it is used in the book and forward the list to parents, who will be asked to give written permission for their children to read the material.

Challenged at the Mechanicsburg, Pennsylvania, Area School District (1992) because of profanity and references to witchcraft.

Challenged as suitable curriculum material in the Harwinton and Burlington, Connecticut, schools (1986) because it contains language and subject matter that set bad examples and give students negative views of life.

Challenged as sixth-grade recommended reading in the Lincoln, Nebraska, schools (1986) because it contains "profanity" including the phrase "Oh, Lord" and "Lord" used as an expletive.

Reviews

Booklist 74 (Nov. 15, 1977): 554.

Bulletin of the Center for Children's Books 31 (Dec. 1977): 66.

Horn Book 54 (Feb. 1978): 48.

School Library Journal 24 (Nov. 1977): 61.

School Librarian 27 (June 1979): 165.

Articles about This Book

Gage, Marilyn Kay. "Katherine Paterson." (projects for nine of her books) *School Library Media Activities Monthly* 8 (Nov. 1991): 26–29.

Hass, Elizabeth, and Patricia Light. "Reading about Death." *Parents* 60 (Aug. 1985): 74–75.

Awards and Prizes

Lewis Carroll Shelf Award, 1978

Michigan Young Reader's Award, Division Two runner-up, 1980

Newbery Medal Award, 1978

Notable Children's Book, 1977

School Library Journal's Best Books of the Year, 1977

References about the Author

Children's Literature Review. Detroit: Gale, 1984. v. 7, pp. 224–43.

Contemporary Authors. Detroit: Gale, 1977. v. 21–24, p. 662.

Contemporary Authors, New Revision Series. Detroit: Gale, 1990. v. 28, pp. 359–64.

Contemporary Literary Criticism. Detroit: Gale, 1980. v. 30, pp. 282–87; v. 12, p. 485.

Dictionary of Literary Biography. Detroit: Gale, 1986. v. 52, pp. 296–314.

Something about the Author. Detroit: Gale, 1988. v. 53, pp. 118–28; v. 13, pp. 176–77.

Sources Recommending This Book

Children's Catalog. 16th ed. Ed. Juliette Yaakov. New York: H. W. Wilson, 1991.

Colborn, Candy. *What Do Children Read Next? A Reader's Guide to Fiction for Children.* Detroit: Gale, 1994.

Donavin, Denise Perry. *Best of the Best for Children.* Chicago: American Library Association, 1992.

Estes, Sally, ed. *Growing Up Is Hard to Do.* Chicago: American Library Association, 1994.

Freeman, Judy. *Books Kids Will Sit Still For: The Complete Read-Aloud Guide.* 2nd ed. New York: R. R. Bowker, 1990.

Gillespie, John T. *The Elementary School Paperback Collection.* Chicago: American Library Association, 1985.

Gillespie, John T. *The Junior High School Paperback Collection.* Chicago: American Library Association, 1985.

Gillespie, John T., and Christine Gilbert, eds. *Best Books for Children: Preschool through the Middle Grades.* 3rd ed. New York: R. R. Bowker, 1985.

Junior High School Library Catalog. 16th ed. Ed. Juliette Yaakov. New York: H. W. Wilson, 1990.

Lee, Lauren K., ed. *The Elementary School Library Collection: A Guide to Books and Other Media.* 18th ed. Williamsport, Pa.: Brodart, 1992.

Middle and Junior High School Library Catalog. 7th ed. Ed. Ann Price and Juliette Yaakov. New York: H. W. Wilson, 1995.

Rochman, Hazel. *Against Borders: Promoting Books for a Multicultural World.* Chicago: American Library Association, 1993.

Rudman, Marsha Kabakow, Kathleen Dunne Gagne, and Joanne E. Berstein. *Books to Help Children Cope with Separation and Loss: An Annotated Bibliography.* 4th ed. New Providence, N.J.: R. R. Bowker, 1993.

The Young Adult Reader's Adviser: The Best in Social Sciences, History, Science and Health. Vol. 2. Ed. Myra Immell. New Providence, N.J.: R. R. Bowker, 1992.

The Great Gilly Hopkins

New York: T. Y. Crowell, 1978

Gilly—short for Tolkien's Galadriel—a foster child, abandoned long ago by her California-bound flower-child mother, has been bounced around from one foster home to the next. Gilly is intelligent, bright, cool, and scheming all at the same time. Placed in Maime Trotter's residence, for what she hopes will be a short stay, Gilly finds her new foster home so unappealing she begins stealing money from Mr. Randolph, a highly independent blind man who lives next to the Trotter residence. Gilly also undertakes a letter-writing campaign to her mother, which results in the appearance of her grandmother, a grandmother she didn't even know existed. Gilly eventually goes to live with her grandmother.

During her time at Maime Trotter's, Gilly expects to continue with her usual foster home behavior, but something changes. Gilly's experiences with Maime; William Ernest, another child in Maime's house; and Mr. Randolph teach her what it means to care for others. She eventually realizes that the large, untidy Trotter house is actually a house full of wisdom and love.

Booklist wrote that "this perceptive story draws strength from its finely delineated characters and rich, moving narrative."

The book was adapted for television.

Challenges

Challenged at the Walnut Elementary School, in Emporia, Kansas (1993), by parents who said that it contained profanity and graphic violence.

Challenged at the Alamo Heights, Texas, School District elementary schools (1992) because it contains the words "hell" and "damn."

Pulled, but later restored, to the language arts curriculum at four Cheshire, Connecticut, elementary schools (1991) because the book is "filled with profanity, blasphemy and obscenities, and gutter language."

Reviews

Booklist 74 (March 15, 1978): 1194.

Bulletin of the Center for Children's Books 31 (May 1978): 146.

Catholic Library World 50 (Nov. 1978): 180.

Horn Book 54 (June 1978): 279.

Publishers Weekly 213 (Feb. 13, 1978): 127.

Publishers Weekly 215 (June 18, 1979): 94.

Publishers Weekly 224 (Dec. 2, 1983): 89.

School Librarian 27 (Dec. 1979): 383.

School Library Journal 24 (April 1978): 87.

Articles about This Book

Elleman, Barbara. "*Learning*'s Summer Reading for Children." *Learning* 12 (April/May 1984): 72.

Sharp, Pat. "Foster Care in Books for Children." *School Library Journal* 30 (Feb. 1984): 28–31.

Background

Paterson, Katherine. "Hope Is More than Happiness." (endings to stories for children) *New York Times Book Review* 93 (Dec. 25, 1988): 19.

Paterson, Katherine. "Living in a Peaceful World." (equipping children to grow toward wholeness and peace) *Horn Book* 67 (Jan./Feb. 1991): 32–38.

Paterson, Katherine. "People I Have Known." *The Writer* 100 (April 1987): 22–24.

Paterson, Katherine. *The Spying Heart: More Thoughts on Reading and Writing Books for Children*. New York: Lodestar Books, 1988.

Schmidt, Gary D. *Katherine Paterson*. New York: Twayne, 1993.

"Waxing Creative." (inspirations of children's authors and illustrators) *Publishers Weekly* 242 (July 17, 1995): 138–41.

Awards and Prizes

American Book Award, 1980

Garden State Children's Book Award for Younger Fiction from the New Jersey Library Association, 1981

Iowa Children's Choice Award from Iowa Educational Media Association, 1981

Jane Addams Peace Association Children's Book Award Honor Book, 1979

National Book Award for Children's Literature, 1979

Newbery Medal Award Honor Book, 1979

School Library Journal's Best Books of the Year, 1978

References about the Author

Children's Literature Review. Detroit: Gale, 1984. v. 7, pp. 224–43.

Contemporary Authors. Detroit: Gale, 1977. v. 21–24, p. 662.

Contemporary Authors, New Revision Series. Detroit: Gale, 1990. v. 28, pp. 359–64.

Contemporary Literary Criticism. Detroit: Gale, 1980. v. 30, pp. 283, 285, 287; v. 12, pp. 486–87.

Dictionary of Literary Biography. Detroit: Gale, 1986. v. 52, pp. 296–314.

Something about the Author. Detroit: Gale, 1988. v. 53, pp. 118–28; v. 13, pp. 176–77.

Sources Recommending This Book

Children's Catalog. 16th ed. Ed. Juliette Yaakov. New York: H. W. Wilson, 1991.

Colborn, Candy. *What Do Children Read Next? A Reader's Guide to Fiction for Children.* Detroit: Gale, 1994.

Gillespie, John T. *The Elementary School Paperback Collection.* Chicago: American Library Association, 1985.

Gillespie, John T. *The Junior High School Paperback Collection.* Chicago: American Library Association, 1985.

Gillespie, John T., and Christine Gilbert, eds. *Best Books for Children: Preschool through the Middle Grades.* 3rd ed. New York: R. R. Bowker, 1985.

Junior High School Library Catalog. 16th ed. Ed. Juliette Yaakov. New York: H. W. Wilson, 1990.

Lee, Lauren K., ed. *The Elementary School Library Collection: A Guide to Books and Other Media.* 18th ed. Williamsport, Pa.: Brodart, 1992.

Middle and Junior High School Library Catalog. 7th ed. Ed. Ann Price and Juliette Yaakov. New York: H. W. Wilson, 1995.

The Young Adult Reader's Adviser: The Best in Social Sciences, History, Science and Health. Vol. 2. Ed. Myra Immel. New Providence, N.J.: R. R. Bowker, 1992.

Boys and Sex

3rd ed. New York: Delacorte Press, 1991

An update of the original, now considered a classic, this publication provides information on a wide variety of human sexuality issues. Presented in a clear, factual, and easy-to-understand style, the author addresses current issues such as homosexuality, AIDS, sexually transmitted diseases, and birth control.

Strides are made to provide information in a nonjudgmental manner. The author relies on the presentation of facts, including extensive information about the human reproduction system, and describes potential consequences of sexual activity such as pregnancy and sexually transmitted diseases.

One glaring inaccuracy mars the authoritativeness of the book: the statement, "Even so, washing after intercourse is at least some precaution against AIDS," is presented in the chapter entitled, "The Real Thing." When the error was discovered, the author requested this statement be stricken from library copies and the publisher reissued the third edition.

To discuss specific topics that are not covered in the book, a question-and-answer chapter concludes the text. Although the book does not include illustrations or diagrams, a concise index and list of books for further reading appends the work.

Doris Fong writes in *School Library Journal,* "Both books are highly readable and should be a part of well-balanced YA collections."

Challenges

Because the book, according to a library critic, urges preadolescent boys and girls to experiment with multiple sexual partners, the book was cited in a move by Gwinnett-Forsyth Regional Library, Georgia, commissioners to label "explicit" library materials and restrict them to readers over age 17, in 1995.

Pulled from the Rangely, Colorado, Middle School Library shelves, in 1994.

Pulled from the Black River Falls, Wisconsin, Middle School Library (1990) because the book "dealt with bestiality, masturbation and homosexuality, and endorsed pre-adolescent and premarital sex."

Because the book "promotes prostitution, promiscuity, homosexuality, and bestiality," the book was removed from two middle-school libraries in Greece, New York, in 1988.

Challenged at the Santa Fe, New Mexico, High School Library (1983) by a school librarian because of its "sordid, suggestive, permissive type of approach."

Reviews

Bulletin of the Center for Children's Books 44 (July 1991): 272.

School Library Journal 37 (June 1991): 132.

Articles about This Book

Campbell, Patty. "The Young Adult Perplex." *Wilson Library Bulletin* 56 (Jan. 1982): 370–71.

References about the Author

Contemporary Authors. Detroit: Gale, 1967. v. 1–4, p. 763.

Contemporary Authors, New Revision Series. Detroit: Gale, 1981. v. 1, pp. 511–12.

Sources Recommending This Book

Dunbar, Linda. "The EL Buying Guide: Human Sexuality K–12." *Emergency Librarian* 16 (Sept./Oct. 1988): 58–59.

Gillespie, John T., ed. *Best Books for Junior High Readers.* New Providence, N.J.: R. R. Bowker, 1991.

Gillespie, John T. *The Junior High School Paperback Collection.* Chicago: American Library Association, 1985.

Gillespie, John T., and Christine Gilbert, eds. *Best Books for Children: Preschool through the Middle Grades.* 3rd ed. New York: R. R. Bowker, 1985.

McGrath, Joan. "Paperbacks for Young Adults." *Emergency Librarian* 9 (April 1982): 28–29.

The Young Adult Reader's Adviser: The Best in Social Sciences, History, Science and Health. Vol. 2. Ed. Myra Immell. New Providence, N.J.: R. R. Bowker, 1992.

Girls and Sex

3rd ed. New York: Delacorte Press, 1991

Because much has changed in the "sexual revolution" since this classic book on sex education was first published in 1969, a third edition was written to address the needs of young girls living in the nineties. This quality book continues to provide adolescent girls with valuable, detailed information on topics such as reproductive systems, dating, homosexuality, falling and being in love, AIDS, other sexually transmitted diseases, pregnancy, and masturbation. The writing style is authoritative, straightforward, and nonjudgmental.

Pomeroy, an authority in the field of human sexual behavior, presents factual information in a clear manner that parallels discussions of the feelings, emotions, attitudes, responsibilities, and consequences of sexual activity. Societal attitudes, including parental and religious ones, are interspersed throughout this contemporary, refreshing look at the sexuality of young girls.

This readable, honest appraisal of the sexual awakening of adolescent girls presents them with the information they want to know as well as the reassurance to help them through this difficult time in their lives.

As with the *Boys* edition, to discuss specific topics that are not covered in the book, a question-and-answer chapter concludes the book. Although the book does not include illustrations or diagrams, a concise index and a list of books for further reading appends the work.

When the first edition was published in 1969, Margaret A. Dorsey praised this ground-breaking book in a review for *Library Journal:* Pomeroy "has now written the most frank and objective book on the subject (of girls' sexual development) presently available for adolescent girls. His book succeeds in doing that better than any other currently available. . . ."

Shirley Everett-Clark, in the June 1992 issue of *Voice of Youth Advocates,* wrote, "*Girls and Sex* will continue to be an important contribution to sexuality literature amongst many other fine publications currently available."

Challenges

Pulled from the Rangely, Colorado, Middle School Library shelves, in 1994.

Pulled from the Black River Falls, Wisconsin, Middle School Library (1990) because the book "dealt with bestiality, masturbation and homosexuality, and endorsed pre-adolescent and premarital sex."

Challenged at the Santa Fe, New Mexico, High School Library (1983) by a school librarian because of its "sordid, suggestive, permissive type of approach."

Reviews

Bulletin of the Center for Children's Books 44 (July 1991): 272.

School Library Journal 37 (June 1991): 132.

Articles about This Book

Campbell, Patty. "The Young Adult Perplex." *Wilson Library Bulletin* 56 (Jan. 1982): 370–71.

References about the Author

Contemporary Authors. Detroit: Gale, 1967. v. 1–4, p. 763.

Contemporary Authors, New Revision Series. Detroit: Gale, 1981. v. 1, pp. 511–12.

Sources Recommending This Book

Dunbar, Linda. "The EL Buying Guide: Human Sexuality K–12." *Emergency Librarian* 16 (Sept./Oct. 1988): 58–59.

Gillespie, John T., ed. *Best Books for Junior High Readers.* New Providence, N.J.: R. R. Bowker, 1991.

Gillespie, John T. *The Junior High School Paperback Collection.* Chicago: American Library Association, 1985.

Gillespie, John T., and Christine Gilbert, eds. *Best Books for Children: Preschool through the Middle Grades.* 3rd ed. New York: R. R. Bowker, 1985.

McGrath, Joan. "Paperbacks for Young Adults." *Emergency Librarian* 9 (April 1982): 28–29.

The Young Adult Reader's Adviser: The Best in Social Sciences, History, Science and Health. Vol. 2. Ed. Myra Immell. New Providence, N.J.: R. R. Bowker, 1992.

LOUIS SACHAR

The Boy Who Lost His Face

New York: Knopf, 1989

Wanting to be a member of the popular, in-crowd, David joins Roger, Scott, and Randy in committing a cruel prank. They pretend to befriend old Mrs. Bayfield, who they think is a witch; but instead they steal her cane, knock her and her rocking chair over, pour lemonade over her face, and throw the empty pitcher through a window. As they are running away from the crime scene, David flips off the old woman. She screams, and it sounds to David like a curse.

David comes to believe that Mrs. Bayfield has put a curse on him because everything that happened to her when the boys victimized her is now happening to him. He cannot do anything right and continues to blame his behavior and the things that occur to him on the curse.

David becomes friends with a new boy in town, Larry, and Mo, a girl from his shop class. At first, the three feel like they are outsiders but gradually realize that Roger, Scott, and Randy are the ones who are really the jerks.

David does have a conscience and moral convictions. From the moment the crime is committed, David feels guilty about his part in the incident. Within his mind, he continually questions his behavior and toys with the idea of apologizing to Mrs. Bayfield. As he gains self-confidence and learns to trust his own judgment, David knows that an apology to Mrs. Bayfield is necessary. When he does apologize to her, she asks him to get her cane back for her. David gets the cane back from Roger, even though a fight ensues. David thinks that the curse will be lifted when he returns the cane. But on his visit to give the cane back, he discovers that Mrs. Bayfield is not a witch, nor did she put a curse on him.

This contemporary, realistic novel accurately portrays the feelings of alienation, acceptance, love, and friendship experienced by young people as they travel through adolescence, which is a most difficult time in their lives.

Challenges

Removed from the Jackson Township Elementary School, in Clay City, Indiana (1993), due to "unsuitable words."

Challenged at the Golden View Elementary School, in San Ramon, California (1993), because of its profanity, frequent use of obscene gestures, and other inappropriate subject matter.

Removed from the Cuyler Elementary School, in Red Creek, New York (1993), because "the age level and use of some swear words may make it inappropriate to younger children."

Challenged at the Thousand Oaks, California, Library (1991) because of inappropriate language.

Reviews

Booklist 86 (Nov. 15, 1989): 675.

Children's Book Review Service 18 (Nov. 1989): 36.

Horn Book 1 (July 1989): 79.

References about the Author

Children's Literature Review. Detroit: Gale, 1992. v. 28, p. 200–205.

Contemporary Authors. Detroit: Gale, 1979. v. 81–84, p. 491.

Contemporary Authors, New Revision Series. Detroit: Gale, 1991. v. 33, p. 386; v. 15, p. 389.

Something about the Author. Detroit: Gale, 1991. v. 63, pp. 137–40; v. 50, p. 188.

ALVIN SCHWARTZ

Scary Stories to Tell in the Dark

New York: HarperCollins, 1981

The book is a wonderful collection of eerie, ghostly, and spine-chilling tales gathered from folklore and retold by the author. Included are stories of ghosts and witches, scary songs, and some of the most popular, funny, and cleverly told stories in this genre today. Contemporary and classic stories are blended with more lighthearted ones. This collection of scary stories is bound to do just that—scare.

The first chapter contains stories to make the listeners of the tales "jump." Other chapters include stories to make an audience laugh and stories about living ghosts. Also included are sections outlining sources, a bibliography, and related articles, all bound to intrigue anyone interested in the history of telling folktales throughout history.

The text is complemented by the marvelously dramatic, chilling, and horror-inspiring pencil illustrations by Caldecott Award–winner, Stephen Gammell. These drawings add a special scary dimension to the already scary text.

This book (along with the others in the series) remains among the most popular for children, and most challenged.

Challenges

Restricted to students in the fourth grade or higher in Enfield, Connecticut, elementary school libraries, in 1995.

Challenged at the Evergreen School District libraries in Vancouver, Washington (1994), because "This book . . . is far beyond other scary books."

Removed from Vancouver, Washington, School District elementary school libraries, in 1994, after surviving two previous attempts, in 1991 and 1993.

Challenged by a parent of a student at Happy Valley Elementary School in Glasgow, Kentucky (1993), who thought it was too scary.

Restricted access at the Marana, Arizona, Unified School District (1993) because of complaints about violence and cannibalism.

Challenged at the elementary school library in Union County, Indiana, in 1992.

Challenged at the West Hartford, Connecticut, elementary and middle-school libraries (1992) because of violence and the subject matter.

Challenged at the Lake Washington School District in Kirkland, Washington (1992), as unacceptably violent for children.

Challenged at the Neely Elementary School in Gilbert, Arizona (1992), because the book shows the dark side

37

of religion through the occult, the devil, and Satanism.

Reviews

Booklist 78 (Dec. 15, 1981): 552.

Bulletin of the Center for Children's Books 35 (June 1982): 1982.

Horn Book 58 (Feb. 1982): 58.

School Library Journal 28 (Jan. 1982): 81.

Articles about This Book

Jones, Patrick. "Have No Fear: Scary Stories for the Middle Grades." *Emergency Librarian* 21 (Sept./Oct. 1993): 30–32.

Background

Dunleavy, M. P. "Children's Writers Plumb the Depths of Fear." *Publishers Weekly* 242 (March 27, 1995): 28–29.

Schwartz, Alvin. "Children, Humor and Folklore." *Catholic Library World* 59 (Sept./Oct. 1987): 67–70.

Awards and Prizes

Arizona Children's Book Award, 1986

References about the Author

Children's Literature Review. Detroit: Gale, 1978. v. 3, pp. 187–93.

Contemporary Authors. Detroit: Gale, 1975. v. 13–16, p. 709.

Contemporary Authors, New Revision Series. Gale, 1992. v. 137, p. 405; v. 24, pp. 419–21; v. 7, pp. 431–32.

Something about the Author. Detroit: Gale, 1993. v. 71, p. 171; v. 56, pp. 145–51; v. 4, pp. 183–84.

Sources Recommending This Book

Carter, Betty, prep. "Teaching through Literature." *Booklist* 86 (May 1, 1990): 1697.

Children's Catalog. 16th ed. Ed. Juliette Yaakov. New York: H. W. Wilson, 1991.

Freeman, Judy. *Books Kids Will Sit Still For: The Complete Read-Aloud Guide.* 2nd ed. New York: R. R. Bowker, 1990.

Gillespie, John T., ed. *Best Books for Junior High Readers.* New Providence, N.J.: R. R. Bowker, 1991.

Gillespie, John T., and Christine Gilbert, eds. *Best Books for Children: Preschool through the Middle Grades.* 3rd ed. New York: R. R. Bowker, 1985.

Junior High School Library Catalog. 16th ed. Ed. Juliette Yaakov. New York: H. W. Wilson, 1990.

Middle and Junior High School Library Catalog. 7th ed. Ed. Ann Price and Juliette Yaakov. New York: H. W. Wilson, 1995.

Zvirin, Stephanie. "Before Stephen King." (scary tales for children) *Booklist* 91 (Jan. 1, 1995): 830–31.

More Scary Stories to Tell in the Dark

New York: HarperCollins, 1984

In this sequel to *Scary Stories to Tell in the Dark*, Schwartz expands on the topics of the first book, tackling subjects not previously addressed. Included in this collection are chapters on ghost stories, stories about "dangerous" places, and stories that are scary and funny.

Back again for this second go-around are the eerie drawings from Stephen Gammell that perfectly complement these tales of terror. Like the first in the series, this collection of stories continues the popularity of Schwartz as a reteller of scary tales for children. Notes and sources, a bibliography, and related articles are once again included for those wanting to do further research on the folktales presented.

Carolyn Camper wrote in *School Library Journal:* "Not since Schwartz' first collection of ghost stories (*Scary Stories to Tell in the Dark*, Lippincott, 1981) has there been a collection of horror stories as well suited for children."

Challenges

Challenged, but retained, as part of a district reading list in Harper Woods, Michigan, in 1995.

Restricted to students in the fourth grade or higher in Enfield, Connecticut, elementary school libraries, in 1995.

Challenged, but retained, at the Whittier Elementary School Library in Bozeman, Montana, in 1994. The book was challenged because it would cause children to fear the dark, have nightmares, and give them an unrealistic view of death.

Challenged at the Evergreen School District libraries in Vancouver, Washington (1994), because "This book . . . is far beyond other scary books."

Removed from Vancouver, Washington, School District elementary school libraries, in 1994, after surviving two previous attempts, in 1991 and 1993.

Restricted access at the Marana, Arizona, Unified School District (1993) because of complaints about violence and cannibalism.

Challenged at the Lake Washington School District in Kirkland, Washington (1992), as unacceptably violent for children.

Challenged at the Neely Elementary School in Gilbert, Arizona (1992), because the book shows the dark side of religion through the occult, the devil, and Satanism.

Challenged at the Dry Hollow Elementary School in The Dalles, Oregon (1988), because it is too scary and violent.

Reviews

Booklist 81 (March 1, 1985): 989.

Bulletin of the Center for Children's Books 38 (Feb. 1985): 116.

Horn Book 61 (March 1985): 183.

School Library Journal 31 (Feb. 1985): 801.

Voice of Youth Advocates 8 (April 1985): 51.

Articles about This Book

Jones, Patrick. "Have No Fear: Scary Stories for the Middle Grades." *Emergency Librarian* 21 (Sept./Oct. 1993): 30–32.

Background

Dunleavy, M. P. "Children's Writers Plumb the Depths of Fear." *Publishers Weekly* 242 (March 27, 1995): 28–29.

Schwartz, Alvin, "Children, Humor and Folklore." *Catholic Library World* 59 (Sept./Oct. 1987): 67–70.

References about the Author

Children's Literature Review. Detroit: Gale, 1978. v. 3, pp. 187–93.

Contemporary Authors. Detroit: Gale, 1975. v. 13–16, p. 709.

Contemporary Authors, New Revision Series. Gale, 1992. v. 137, p. 405; v. 24, pp. 419–21; v. 7, pp. 431–32.

Something about the Author. Detroit: Gale, 1993. v. 71, p. 171; v. 56, pp. 145–51; v. 4, pp. 183–84.

Sources Recommending This Book

Children's Catalog. 16th ed. Ed. Juliette Yaakov. New York: H. W. Wilson, 1991.

Gillespie, John T., ed. *Best Books for Junior High Readers.* New Providence, N.J.: R. R. Bowker, 1991.

Junior High School Library Catalog. 16th ed. Ed. Juliette Yaakov. New York: H. W. Wilson, 1990.

Middle and Junior High School Library Catalog. 7th ed. Ed. Ann Price and Juliette Yaakov. New York: H. W. Wilson, 1995.

Zvirin, Stephanie. "Before Stephen King." (scary tales for children) *Booklist* 91 (Jan. 1, 1995): 830–31.

Scary Stories 3: More Tales to Chill Your Bones

New York: HarperCollins, 1991

Once again reuniting the team of Alvin Schwartz, as reteller of the tales, and Stephen Gammell, whose black-and-white pen-and-ink drawings perfectly complement the tales presented, *Scary Stories 3* is different from the previous two collections in that most of the stories presented here "may have at least a little truth, for strange things sometimes happen, and people love to tell about them and turn them into even better stories."

The stories include traditional tales of ghosts, witches, and severed hands. Short chapters include "When Death Arrives," "On the Edge," "Running Wild," "Five Nightmares," "What Is Going on Here?" and "Whooooooooo?"

As with the two previous collections, extensive source notes detailing the origins of the tales, a bibliography, and related articles are included for further research.

Molly Kinney, reviewing for *School Library Journal*, wrote "Scary Stories 3 is here! And it was worth the wait. . . . This will be a well-used addition to all collections."

Challenges

Challenged at the Evergreen School District libraries in Vancouver, Washington (1994), because "This book . . . is far beyond other scary books."

Removed from Vancouver, Washington, School District elementary school libraries, in 1994, after surviving two previous attempts, in 1991 and 1993.

Challenged at the West Hartford, Connecticut, elementary and middle-school libraries (1992) because of violence and the subject matter.

Challenged at the Lake Washington School District in Kirkland, Washington (1992), as unacceptably violent for children.

Reviews

Booklist 87 (Aug. 1991): 2146.

Bulletin of the Center for Children's Books 45 (Dec. 1991): 105.

Horn Book 67 (Nov. 1991): 749.

Publishers Weekly 238 (Aug. 9, 1991): 58.

Articles about This Book

Jones, Patrick. "Have No Fear: Scary Stories for the Middle Grades." *Emergency Librarian* 21 (Sept./ Oct. 1993): 30–32.

Background

Dunleavy, M. P. "Children's Writers Plumb the Depths of Fear." *Publishers Weekly* 242 (March 27, 1995): 28–29.

Schwartz, Alvin. "Children, Humor and Folklore." *Catholic Library World* 59 (Sept./Oct. 1987): 67–70.

References about the Author

Children's Literature Review. Detroit: Gale, 1978. v. 3, pp. 187–93.

Contemporary Authors. Detroit: Gale, 1975. v. 13–16, p. 709.

Contemporary Authors, New Revision Series. Gale, 1992. v. 137, p. 405; v. 24, pp. 419–21; v. 7, pp. 431–32.

Something about the Author. Detroit: Gale, 1993. v. 71, p. 171; v. 56, pp. 145–51; v. 4, pp. 183–84.

Sources Recommending This Book

Freeman, Judy. *More Books Kids Will Sit Still For.* New Providence, N.J.: R. R. Bowker, 1995.

Higgs, Jessica. "Fact or Fiction? Books Which Celebrate the Unexplained." *Emergency Librarian* 20 (Jan. 1993): 53.

Middle and Junior High School Library Catalog. 7th ed. Ed. Ann Price and Juliette Yaakov. New York: H. W. Wilson, 1995.

Zvirin, Stephanie. "Before Stephen King." (scary tales for children) *Booklist* 91 (Jan. 1, 1995): 830–31.

MAURICE SENDAK

In the Night Kitchen

New York: Harper & Row, 1970

In a dream, Mickey floats through the night sky, arriving at the Night Kitchen. He lands in a bowl of unfinished cake batter. Mistaking Mickey for the final ingredient—milk—the three bakers continue stirring the batter. He then skips into a batch of rising bread dough. After kneading it to baking consistency, Mickey makes an airplane out of the mixture. He flies up into the night sky, tumbles out of the airplane, and falls into a giant milk bottle. Mickey pours some milk into the unfinished batter. The bakers are delighted that they've finally been given the missing ingredient. They mix the batter, beat the batter, and put it in the oven to bake. By daybreak, Mickey is back in his own bed—asleep, "cake-free and dried." He wakes up knowing how he is able to have "cake every morning" for breakfast.

This surrealistic fantasy-dream is set against a clever and imaginative city skyline that has been built using a wide variety of cooking utensils and kitchen containers, including jars, cartons, cans, boxes, and even salt-and-pepper shakers.

The perfect combination of a text based in the literary tradition of nursery rhymes and illustrations executed in a 1930-ish, art-deco style evokes the comforting smells and decor of a homey, family kitchen.

Although acclaimed by many, this picture book initially was received with cries of outrage because of Sendak's blatant use of nudity and exploration of a child's sexuality.

Since the book was first published, "concerned" librarians, teachers, and parents have taken the liberty of dressing Mickey in diapers or pants by drawing over pictures of his unclothed body.

Certainly ahead of its time, this early work of Sendak's remains a favorite of children.

Challenges

Challenged at the El Paso, Texas, Public Library (1994) because "the little boy pictured did not have any clothes on and it pictured his private area."

Because reading the book "could lay the foundation for future use of pornography," the book was challenged at the Elk River, Minnesota, schools, in 1992.

Challenged at the Camden, New Jersey, elementary school libraries because of nudity, in 1989.

Challenged at the Robeson Elementary School, in Champaign, Illinois (1988), because of "gratuitous" nudity.

Reviews

Booklist 67 (Jan. 15, 1971): 423.

Bulletin of the Center for Children's Books 24 (Jan. 1971): 80.

Horn Book 47 (Feb. 1971): 44.

Library Journal 95 (Dec. 15, 1970): 4341.

Articles about This Book

Elswit, Sharon. "Bedtime Books for Bedtime." *School Library Journal* 26 (March 1980): 104–5.

Background

Nickerson, Mary. "Princess Moaning Minnie, Mrs. Coalsack, and Muggle-Wump Meet Randy Monroe." *School Library Journal* 27 (Oct. 1980): 118–19.

Sadler, Glen Edward. "Maurice Sendak and Dr. Seuss: A Conversation." *Horn Book* 65 (Sept./Oct. 1989): 582–88.

Sendak, Maurice. "The Coming Together of All My Various Worlds." *Top of the News* 26 (June 1970): 366–69.

Awards and Prizes

Art Books for Children Award, 1973, 1974, and 1975

Caldecott Medal Award Honor Book, 1971

Chandler Book Talk Reward of Merit, 1967

Hans Christian Andersen Award, for body of his illustration work, 1970

Notable Children's Book, 1970

Redbook Award, 1985

School Library Journal's Best Books of the Year, 1970

References about the Author

Children's Literature Review. Detroit: Gale, 1989. v. 17, pp. 93–129; v. 1, pp. 166–73.

Contemporary Authors. Detroit: Gale, 1969. v. 5–8, p. 1035.

Contemporary Authors, New Revision Series. Detroit: Gale, 1992. v. 39, pp. 354–61; v. 11, pp. 457–65.

Something about the Author. Detroit: Gale, 1982. v. 27, pp. 181–201; v. 1, pp. 190–91.

Sources Recommending This Book

Children's Catalog. 16th ed. Ed. Juliette Yaakov. New York: H. W. Wilson, 1991.

Donavin, Denise Perry. *Best of the Best for Children.* Chicago: American Library Association, 1992.

Gillespie, John T., and Christine Gilbert, eds. *Best Books for Children: Preschool through the Middle Grades.* 3rd ed. New York: R. R. Bowker, 1985.

Lee, Lauren K., ed. *The Elementary School Library Collection: A Guide to Books and Other Media.* 18th ed. Williamsport, Pa.: Brodart, 1992.

Sutherland, Zena. *The Best in Children's Books.* Chicago: University of Chicago Press, 1991.

SHEL SILVERSTEIN

A Light in the Attic

New York: Harper & Row, 1981

In this witty, original collection of poems by the author of the ever-popular *Where the Sidewalk Ends,* young readers meet a cast of interesting, wacky characters and read about many unusual, strange happenings. The poems vary in length, style, and humor-level. They are ideally complemented with stark black line drawings.

A few of the poems revisit familiar nursery rhymes, such as "Rockabye," in which the narrator questions why anyone would put a baby and its cradle in a treetop. Spin-offs of well-known fairy tales are evident in several poems, including "Picture Puzzle Piece," "Captain Blackbeard Did What?" and "In Search of Cinderella." Children will definitely relate to their peers in poems such as "How Not to Have to Dry the Dishes," "Prayer of a Selfish Child," and "Little Abigail and the Beautiful Pony." Some poems, including "Whatifs" and "The Little Boy and the Old Man," explore the more–sensitive feelings of children. But most of the poems are downright silly and nonsensical. The collection is perfect for reading aloud and will tickle the funny bones of young listeners and readers alike.

Adults may have difficulties with many of the questionable topics featured in these poems. The irreverent subjects include a babysitter who sits on the baby she's caring for, damsels who are eaten by the Dragon of Grindly Grun, nudity shown in several illustrations, people drowning, bodies having missing parts, a child's death because her parents refused to buy her a pony, and possible disrespect to God.

In spite of parental concern about these and other poems that are anthologized in this book, *A Light in the Attic* has vast child-appeal. Professional book reviewers have praised this entertaining and humorous poetry collection. Since its publication in 1981, libraries across the country rarely have had copies of this book sitting on shelves due to the book's immense popularity and the high demand from youngsters everywhere.

Challenges

Challenged at the Fruitland Park Elementary School Library, in Lake County, Florida (1993), because the book "promotes disrespect, horror, and violence."

Because the poem "Little Abigail and the Beautiful Pony" is morbid, the book was challenged at the West Mifflin, Pennsylvania, schools, in 1992.

Restricted to students with parental permission at the Duval County, Florida, public school libraries (1992) because the book features a caricature of a person whose nude behind has been stung by a bee.

Challenged at the South Adams, Indiana, school libraries (1989) because the book is "very vile" and "contained subliminal or underlying messages and anti-parent material."

Challenged as suitable classroom material because of its "objectionable" nature at the Hot Springs, South Dakota, Elementary School, in 1989.

Because a mother protested that it "exposes children to the horrors of suicide," the poem "Little Abigail and the Beautiful Pony," from this award-winning children's book, was banned from second-grade classes in Huffman, Texas, in 1989.

Challenged at the Morneo Valley, California, Unified School District libraries (1987) because it "contains profanity, sexual situations, and themes that allegedly encourage disrespectful behavior."

Challenged at the Appoquinimink schools in Middletown, Delaware (1987), because the book "contains violence, idealizes death, and makes light of manipulative behavior."

Reviews

Booklist 78 (Dec. 1, 1981): 502.

Bulletin of the Center for Children's Books 35 (Feb. 1982): 117.

Catholic Library World 53 (March 1982): 357.

Kirkus Reviews 50 (Jan. 1, 1982): 10.

Publishers Weekly 220 (Sept. 18, 1981): 155.

School Librarian 31 (March 1983): 73.

School Library Journal 28 (Dec. 1981): 57.

School Library Media Quarterly 10 (Spring 1982): 206.

Voice of Youth Advocates 4 (Feb. 1982): 45.

Background

Livingston, Myra Cohn. "The Light in His Attic." (work of S. Silverstein) *New York Times Book Review* 91 (March 9, 1986): 36–37.

Wallace, Robert. "Light Verse." *The Writer* 98 (Dec. 1985): 20–22.

Awards and Prizes

Buckeye Award, 1983 and 1985

George G. Stone Award, 1984

Notable Children's Recording, 1986

School Library Journal's Best Books of the Year, 1981

William Allen White Award, 1984

References about the Author

Children's Literature Review. Detroit: Gale, 1983. v. 5, pp. 208–13.

Contemporary Authors. Detroit: Gale, 1983. v. 107, pp. 471–72.

Contemporary Authors, New Revision Series. Detroit: Gale, 1995. v. 47, pp. 403–5.

Something about the Author. Detroit: Gale, 1983. v. 33, pp. 210–13; v. 27, p. 202.

Sources Recommending This Book

"Books to Make You Giggle and Grin." *Emergency Librarian* 12 (May/June 1985): 11–12.

Children's Catalog. 16th ed. Ed. Juliette Yaakov. New York: H. W. Wilson, 1991.

Donavin, Denise Perry. *Best of the Best for Children.* Chicago: American Library Association, 1992.

Gillespie, John T., ed. *Best Books for Junior High Readers.* New Providence, N.J.: R. R. Bowker, 1991.

Gillespie, John T., and Christine Gilbert, eds. *Best Books for Children: Preschool through the Middle Grades.* 3rd ed. New York: R. R. Bowker, 1985.

Junior High School Library Catalog. 16th ed. Ed. Juliette Yaakov. New York: H. W. Wilson, 1990.

Lee, Lauren K., ed. *The Elementary School Library Collection: A Guide to Books and Other Media.* 18th ed. Williamsport, Pa.: Brodart, 1992.

Middle and Junior High School Library Catalog. 7th ed. Ed. Ann Price and Juliette Yaakov. New York: H. W. Wilson, 1995.

The Headless Cupid

New York: Atheneum, 1971

When David's father remarried, David knew things were going to change around the house; he just didn't anticipate the arrival of his new, older stepsister. Amanda, a student of witchcraft, arrives dressed in her ceremonial costume and with a black crow she calls her familiar in hand.

Amanda immediately creates conflict within the Stanley household, treating the other children with contempt and being angry with the adults who have changed her life-style so drastically. Amanda, however, soon realizes she has a new "flock" in the children of the house. David's mother had an interest in the occult, which sparks the interest in David and the rest of the children (because David is interested). She subjects the children to a series of "ordeals"—or initiation rites—which culminate with a seance. These ordeals are nothing more than a ploy on Amanda's part to disrupt the household. As the story unfolds, David begins to feel that Amanda may be just a troublemaker, and not the witch she professes to be.

Events take an interesting twist when David and Amanda learn that in 1896 the house was said to be the scene of poltergeist activity, which resulted in the beheading of a carved cupid figure on the stairway. A series of unexplained disturbances add to the unrest, but David soon discovers that the unrest was caused by Amanda.

This fascinating story deals more with the result of blended families than the occult, and many children can relate to the five children, as well as the adults presented.

The *Bulletin of the Center for Children's Books* wrote, "The book is one of the author's most successful, for the plot is free of irrelevancies; as usual, the writing is relaxed and literate, and the characterizations of the five children—and of the parents as well—are excellent."

Challenges

Challenged in the Escondido, California, school (1992) because it contains references to the occult.

Despite objections to its references to witchcraft, the book was retained on the approved reading list at the Matthew Henson Middle School, in Waldorf, Maryland, in 1991.

After a parent objected to the book because it "introduces children to the occult and fantasy about immoral acts," the book was retained in the Grand Haven, Michigan, school libraries, in 1990.

Challenged at the Hays, Kansas, Public Library (1989) because the book "could lead young readers to embrace Satanism."

Reviews

Booklist 68 (Sept. 15, 1971): 110.

Bulletin of the Center for Children's Books 25 (Nov. 1971): 51.

Horn Book 47 (Oct. 1971): 485.

Library Journal 96 (Sept. 15, 1971): 2933.

Publishers Weekly 200 (July 26, 1971): 52.

Background

Karl, Jean. "Zilpha Keatley Snyder." *Elementary English* 51 (Sept. 1974): 785–89.

Awards and Prizes

Christopher Medal, 1972

Hans Christian Andersen Award honor list, 1974

Newbery Medal Award Honor Book, 1972

Notable Children's Book, 1971

William Allen White Award, 1972

References about the Author

Children's Literature Review. Detroit: Gale, 1994. v. 31, pp. 149–70.

Contemporary Authors. Detroit: Gale, 1974. v. 9–12, p. 851.

Contemporary Authors, New Revision Series. Detroit: Gale, 1993. v. 38, pp. 401–5.

Contemporary Literary Criticism. Detroit: Gale, 1981. v. 17, pp. 471–72.

Something about the Author. Detroit: Gale, 1994. v. 75, pp. 190–94; v. 28, pp. 192–94; v. 1, pp. 202–3.

Sources Recommending This Book

Children's Catalog. 16th ed. Ed. Juliette Yaakov. New York: H. W. Wilson, 1991.

Gillespie, John T. *The Elementary School Paperback Collection.* Chicago: American Library Association, 1985.

Gillespie, John T. *The Junior High School Paperback Collection.* Chicago: American Library Association, 1985.

Gillespie, John T., and Christine Gilbert, eds. *Best Books for Children: Preschool through the Middle Grades.* 3rd ed. New York: R. R. Bowker, 1985.

Lee, Lauren K., ed. *The Elementary School Library Collection: A Guide to Books and Other Media.* 18th ed. Williamsport, Pa.: Brodart, 1992.

THEODORE TAYLOR

The Cay

Garden City, N.Y.: Doubleday, 1969

In April of 1942, Phillip and his racist mother are leaving war-time Curaçao by freighter to return to their home in Virginia. When the freighter is torpedoed, Phillip loses consciousness. He awakens on a raft with an old West Indian man, Timothy, and a cat called Stew. Phillip is leery about being stranded with this man in this unexpected, frightening situation because Phillip's mother always told him that she did not like black people. Within a short time, Phillip becomes totally blind due to a head injury received when the freighter was torpedoed.

After a harrowing voyage, they finally land on a tiny cay. Because of his blindness, Phillip is initially dependent on Timothy. Knowing that he is old, tired, and probably close to death, Timothy teaches Phillip life-saving skills as they work together in their never-ending struggle for survival. As weeks pass, Phillip gains increased trust in and admiration for Timothy.

Phillip's blindness blurs the color barrier that he originally imposed upon them. At one point, Phillip asks Timothy if he is still black. Timothy and Phillip discuss the similarities and differences in their lives and eventually come to understand that no matter what color a person's skin is, beneath it everyone is the same.

And when Timothy does die after being injured in a violent hurricane, Phillip realizes for what Timothy was preparing him.

Phillip is finally rescued in August 1942 and reunited with his parents. He vows to return to the "lonely little island where Timothy is buried."

Critics, including the Interracial Council on Children's Books, attacked this novel as being racist. Zena Sutherland, in her review for the *New York Times Book Review* of June 29, 1969, wrote that the story "gains deeper significance after Phillip . . . a caste-conscious product of neo-colonial white society . . . realizes that racial consciousness is merely a product of sight: to him Timothy feels neither white nor black."

Although some young readers will have difficulty reading Timothy's spoken words, the dialect gives his character authenticity. Use of this dialect has also been widely criticized. But a *School Library Journal* starred review stated that Taylor incorporated an "artful, unobtrusive use of dialect" in this novel.

A television adaptation of *The Cay,* starring James Earl Jones, was aired in fall 1974.

Challenges

Because it maligns African Americans, the book was challenged at the Sequoia, California, Junior High School, in 1992. The Moorpark School Board voted 3–1, with one abstention, not to ban the book, denounced as "racist."

Reviews

Book World 3 (May 4, 1969): 36.

Booklist 65 (July 15, 1969): 1277.

Bulletin of the Center for Children's Books 22 (July 1969): 183.

Horn Book 45 (Oct. 1969): 537.

Journal of Reading 22 (Nov. 1978): 127.

Kirkus Reviews 37 (May 15, 1969): 560.

Library Journal 94 (June 15, 1969): 2505.

Publishers Weekly 195 (June 9, 1969): 63.

Background

Hubbard, Kim. "Return to the Cay." *People Weekly* 40 (Dec. 20, 1993): 105–6.

Awards and Prizes

Jane Addams Children's Book Award from Women's International League for Peace and Freedom (returned, 1975)

Lewis Carroll Shelf Award, 1970

Notable Children's Book, 1969

School Library Journal's Best Books of the Year, 1969

References about the Author

Children's Literature Review. Detroit: Gale, 1993. v. 30, pp. 172–97.

Contemporary Authors. Detroit: Gale, 1977. v. 21–24, p. 870.

Contemporary Authors, New Revision Series. Detroit: Gale, 1993. v. 38, pp. 424–27; v. 25, p. 441; v. 9, pp. 491–92.

Something about the Author. Detroit: Gale, 1989. v. 54, pp. 135–46; v. 5, pp. 185–86.

Something about the Author, Autobiography Series. Vol. 4. Detroit: Gale, 1987.

Sources Recommending This Book

Children's Catalog. 16th ed. Ed. Juliette Yaakov. New York: H. W. Wilson, 1991.

Colborn, Candy. *What Do Children Read Next? A Reader's Guide to Fiction for Children.* Detroit: Gale, 1994.

Gillespie, John T., ed. *Best Books for Junior High Readers.* New Providence, N.J.: R. R. Bowker, 1991.

Gillespie, John T. *The Elementary School Paperback Collection.* Chicago: American Library Association, 1985.

Gillespie, John T. *The Junior High School Paperback Collection.*

Chicago: American Library Association, 1985.

Gillespie, John T., and Christine Gilbert, eds. *Best Books for Children: Preschool through the Middle Grades.* 3rd ed. New York: R. R. Bowker, 1985.

Junior High School Library Catalog. 16th ed. Ed. Juliette Yaakov. New York: H. W. Wilson, 1990.

Lee, Lauren K., ed. *The Elementary School Library Collection: A Guide to Books and Other Media.* 18th ed. Williamsport, Pa.: Brodart, 1992.

Middle and Junior High School Library Catalog. 7th ed. Ed. Ann Price and Juliette Yaakov. New York: H. W. Wilson, 1995.

Daddy's Roommate

Boston: Alyson Publications, 1990

Daddy's Roommate, a picture book for young readers, is told from the perspective of a young boy who spends time with his father and his father's partner, Frank, following the divorce of his parents. The two men are portrayed as a loving couple in a realistic way—they "work together, eat together, sleep together, shave together, and sometimes even fight together, but they always make up."

The child tells us about Frank, his father's roommate, showing how much fun they have. Also, he describes the things the three of them do when they are together.

Just as the two men are seen to relate to one another like any other couple, the adventures that the young boy has with Daddy and Frank are the same as any other child might have. When his mother explains that the child's father and Frank love each other, and that is why they live together, the boy responds: "Being gay is just one more kind of love, and love is the best kind of happiness." The boy closes the book with the observation that "Daddy and his roommate are very happy together, and I'm happy too!"

Because the book does a good job expressing the humanity and "normality" of gay people, it is a good choice for schools and libraries wishing to include in their collections books that encourage understanding and confront misconceptions about gays and lesbians. Unfortunately, the critical success of the book also raised its visibility, resulting in more challenges, removals, and reclassifications.

Daddy's Roommate is suited perfectly to its audience, using simple language and bold illustrations to tell the story. As such, it is an effective means by which children can get a glimpse of the truth of mainstream gay life without fear or suspicion. The book is important as well for children who have gay parents—not only does it reflect their own lives, which is always important and empowering, but it can serve as a catalyst for dialogue between these children and their peers. *Daddy's Roommate* expresses beautifully that gay people can love as well and parent as well as anyone else, in a manner that is entirely appropriate to its audience.

Challenges

After more than a month of controversy and debate, trustees of the Rutland, Vermont, Free Library decided, in 1995, not to create a special section for or restrict access to the book.

Removed from the children's section of the Fort Worth, Texas, Public Library (1994) because critics say it legitimizes gay relationships.

Challenged at the Chandler, Arizona, Public Library (1994) because the book is a "skillful presentation to the young child about lesbianism/homosexuality."

Removed by Land County Head Start officials in Cottage Grove, Oregon, from its antibias curriculum, in 1994.

Challenged, but retained, at the Dayton and Montgomery County, Ohio, Public Library, in 1993.

Because it is "vile, sick and goes against every law and constitution," the book was challenged at the Mesa, Arizona, Public Library, in 1993.

Challenged at the Alachua County Library in High Springs, Florida, in 1993.

Challenged at the Seekonk, Massachusetts, Library, in 1993.

Challenged at the North Brunswick, New Jersey, Public Library, in 1993.

Challenged at the Cumberland County, North Carolina, Public Library, in 1993.

Challenged at the Chattanooga-Hamilton County, Tennessee, Bicentennial Library, in 1993.

Challenged at the Wicomico County Free Library in Salisbury, Maryland, in 1993.

Challenged at the Sussex, Wisconsin, Public Library, in 1993.

Challenged at the Juneau, Alaska, school libraries, in 1993.

Moved from the children's section to the adult section at the Manatee, Florida, Public Library, in 1993,

and the Elizabethtown, North Carolina, Library, also in 1993.

Restricted to adults at the Lake Lanier Regional Library System in Gwinnett County, Georgia, in 1993.

Moved from the children's section to the adult section of the Mercer County Library System in Lawrence, New Jersey, in 1993.

Challenged in the Rosemount–Apple Valley School District in Eden, Minnesota, in 1993.

Because it "promotes a dangerous and ungodly lifestyle from which children must be protected," the book was challenged in the Wayne County Public Library, in Goldsboro, North Carolina; the Grand Prairie, Texas, Memorial Library; the Cumberland County Public Library, Fayetteville, North Carolina; and the Tillamook, Oregon, Public Library in 1992.

Challenged (in 1992) at the Roswell Public Library in New Mexico and the Dauphin County Library System in Pennsylvania because the book's intent "is indoctrination into a gay lifestyle."

Challenged at the Timberland Regional Libraries in Olympia, Washington (1992), because the book promotes homosexuality and is offensive.

Removed from the Brooklyn, New York, School District's curriculum (1992) because the school board objected to words that were "age inappropriate."

Reviews

Booklist 87 (March 1, 1991): 1403.
Bulletin of the Center for Children's Books 44 (March 1991): 182.

Publishers Weekly 237 (Dec. 7, 1990): 80.

School Library Journal 37 (April 1991): 105.

Articles about This Book

Loch, Marge Wouters. "Children's Cornucopia: Whose Family's Values? Gay and Lesbian Families in Children's Books." *WLW Journal* 15 (Winter 1992/1993): 13–14.

Background

Ford, Michael Thomas. "Gay Books for Young Readers: When Caution Calls the Shots." *Publishers Weekly* 241 (Feb. 21, 1994): 24–27.

References about the Author

Something about the Author. Detroit: Gale, 1993. v. 71, pp. 213–15.

What ALA Can Do to Help Librarians Combat Censorship

The American Library Association maintains a broad program for the promotion and defense of intellectual freedom, composed of the Intellectual Freedom Committee (IFC); the Office for Intellectual Freedom (OIF); the Intellectual Freedom Round Table (IFRT); the Intellectual Freedom Action Network; the Freedom to Read Foundation; and the LeRoy C. Merritt Humanitarian Fund.

The basic program of the Intellectual Freedom Committee is educational in nature. The most effective safeguards for the rights of library users and librarians are an informed public and a library profession aware of repressive activities and how to combat them. Toward this end, the administrative arm of the Intellectual Freedom Committee, the Office for Intellectual Freedom, implements ALA policies on intellectual freedom and educates librarians about the importance of the concept. The Office for Intellectual Freedom maintains a wide-ranging program of educational and informational publications, projects, and services.

The *Newsletter on Intellectual Freedom,* the official bimonthly publication of the Intellectual Freedom Committee, was initiated in 1952 and has been edited and produced by the OIF staff since 1970. The *Newsletter* is addressed to both librarians and members of the general public concerned about intellectual freedom. Its main purpose is to provide a comprehensive national picture of censorship efforts, court cases, legislation, and current readings on the subject. Through original and reprinted articles, the *Newsletter* offers a forum for expressing varying views about intellectual freedom, while providing a means for reporting activities of the Intellectual Freedom Committee, the Office for Intellectual Freedom, and the Freedom to Read Foundation. In 1982, noted civil liberties authority Nat Hentoff named the *Newsletter* "the best small publication in America." It is available by subscription from the Office for Intellectual Freedom.

Intellectual Freedom Action News is a different publication: a brief,

Adapted in part from the *Intellectual Freedom Manual,* 5th ed., by the Office for Intellectual Freedom (American Library Association, 1996).

informal monthly newsletter designed to provide updates on late-breaking censorship controversies or legislation that could affect intellectual freedom in libraries and to alert members and supporters to areas where they may find additional information or localities where their assistance is needed. The *Action News* serves as the newsletter (both print and electronic) for the Intellectual Freedom Action Network, a grassroots, ad hoc group of volunteers who have identified themselves as willing to come forward in support of the freedom to read in censorship controversies in their communities. It is also circulated to state chapter and divisional intellectual freedom committees, ALA chapter councilors, and others who indicate interest. The *Action News* provides information that may assist network members in the promotion and defense of intellectual freedom, and it gives suggestions for new programs and project ideas.

The Office for Intellectual Freedom also produces and distributes documents, articles, and ALA policies concerning intellectual freedom to both librarians and the general public. Monographs, resource guides, training materials, and manuals include the *Intellectual Freedom Manual,* fifth edition; the anually produced *Banned Books Week Resource Kit; Confidentiality in Libraries: An Intellectual Freedom Modular Education Program;* and *Censorship and Selection: Issues and Answers for Schools* (revised edition, by Henry Reichman). During nationwide controversies concerning individual titles, press clippings, editorials, and public statements detailing the ways various libraries around the country handled requests to remove specific materials are compiled and sent out to others handling similar problems.

One of the most often used and least heard about functions of the Office is its provision of advice and consultation (case support) to individuals in the throes of potential or actual censorship controversies. Rarely does a day go by without a request by phone or letter asking for advice about a specific book, video, or audio recording that has drawn the censorious attention of an individual or group. When asked for assistance, the Office provides reviews and information about the author of the challenged material, applicable ALA policies, advice about the implementation of reconsideration policies, and other counseling specific to the situation at hand. Or, if requested, the Office can provide the names of persons available to offer testimony or support before library boards, supplied from the ranks of the Intellectual Freedom Action Network and state library association intellectual freedom committees. The options chosen are always the prerogative of the individual requesting assistance. If a censorship problem arises, librarians should call Office for Intellectual Freedom (50 East Huron Street, Chicago, IL 60611; (312) 280-4223 or (800) 545-2433, extension 4223).

In 1990, the Office for Intellectual Freedom established a censorship database to record and report statistics on challenges to library materials across the country. The database is a useful tool for identifying trends in types of censorship cases and for documenting responses and solutions to these cases. All librarians are encouraged to document and report challenges—and their outcome—to the Office for Intellectual Freedom. Information about the particular institution, its specific location, and the parties involved are kept confidential until—and only if—the information is published elsewhere. For statistical purposes, and to inform the public of the prevalence of censorship problems in our society, the Office might release only the name of the challenged material and the state in which the challenge occurred.

The Office for Intellectual Freedom welcomes reports in the form of newspaper clippings, magazine articles, cards, and letters.

Of special importance, of course, are the state library association intellectual freedom committees. The extent and nature of the activities of these committees vary from state to state. Some groups are more active than others. In some states, the committees have worked with other organizations to build impressive state coalitions in defense of intellectual and academic freedom. Elsewhere they have concentrated on compiling and developing state intellectual freedom manuals and continuing education materials. The relationship of the ALA Intellectual Freedom Committee and the Office with the state committees is one of mutual cooperation and assistance. The Office supports the work at the state level with information, coordination, and ideas. On their part, the state committees can be the Office's "eyes and ears" at the local level.

Online Resources

With the increased use of the Internet for communicating, the Office for Intellectual Freedom established a "listserv" to allow discussion among persons interested in the issue of intellectual freedom. An unmoderated list, ALAOIF is among the most popular lists currently available.

To subscribe, send the message "subscribe alaoif <your first name> <your last name>" to listproc@ala.org.

The *Library Bill of Rights* along with other American Library Association intellectual freedom policies, can be found on the ALA home page at http://www.ala.org.

Banned Books Week

The event that draws the most attention to the Office for Intellectual Freedom is the yearly celebration, Banned Books Week—Celebrating the

Freedom to Read. Banned Books Week began in 1982 to call attention to the danger of censorship and encourage support for the freedom to read. It is sponsored by the American Library Association and cosponsored by the American Booksellers Association, the American Booksellers Foundation for Free Expression, the Association of American Publishers, the American Society of Journalists and Authors, and the National Association of College Stores. It is also endorsed by the Center for the Book of the Library of Congress.

Each year, in conjunction with Banned Books Week, OIF releases a *Resource Guide* for use by libraries, bookstores, and other organizations. It includes a list of books that have been banned or challenged during the previous year.

The challenges included in the report represent only those that have been reported publicly. No names of parents or others registering complaints are published.

Becoming involved and working together with colleagues and friends, librarians can fulfill their mission to confront censorship and protect access to the broadest range of information.

Number of Challenges Reported to the Office for Intellectual Freedom

The Stupids Step Out—Harry Allard	4
The Indian in the Cupboard—Lynne Reid Banks	4
Blubber—Judy Blume	18
The Goats—Brock Cole	7
My Brother Sam Is Dead—James Lincoln Collier and Christopher Collier	14
James and the Giant Peach—Roald Dahl	5
A Wrinkle in Time—Madeleine L'Engle	4
The Giver—Lois Lowry	12
Halloween ABC—Eve Merriam	15
Heather Has Two Mommies—Leslea Newman	31
Bridge to Terabithia—Katherine Paterson	30
The Great Gilly Hopkins—Katherine Paterson	16
Boys and Sex—Wardell Pomeroy	8
Girls and Sex—Wardell Pomeroy	4
The Boy Who Lost His Face—Louis Sachar	9
Scary Stories to Tell in the Dark—Alvin Schwartz	35
More Scary Stories to Tell in the Dark—Alvin Schwartz	39
Scary Stories 3: More Tales to Chill Your Bones—Alvin Schwartz	14
In the Night Kitchen—Maurice Sendak	19
A Light in the Attic—Shel Silverstein	15
The Headless Cupid—Zilpha Snyder	4
The Cay—Theodore Taylor	6
Daddy's Roommate—Michael Wilhoite	84

The Office for Intellectual Freedom does not claim comprehensiveness in recording challenges. Research suggests that for each challenge reported, as many as four or five are unreported.

Donna Reidy Pistolis is the associate director
for Case Support and Research in the Office for
Intellectual Freedom. She received her MLS from
Northern Illinois University in 1993.